UNIVERSITY PARK
⊰⊱ LOS ANGELES ⊰⊱

A BRIEF HISTORY

CHARLES EPTING

Charleston · London
THE
History
PRESS

Published by The History Press
Charleston, SC 29403
www.historypress.net

Copyright © 2013 by Charles Epting
All rights reserved

Images are courtesy of the author unless otherwise noted.

First published 2013

Manufactured in the United States

ISBN 978.1.60949.960.0

Library of Congress CIP data applied for.

Notice: The information in this book is true and complete to the best of our knowledge. It is offered without guarantee on the part of the author or The History Press. The author and The History Press disclaim all liability in connection with the use of this book.

All rights reserved. No part of this book may be reproduced or transmitted in any form whatsoever without prior written permission from the publisher except in the case of brief quotations embodied in critical articles and reviews.

*This book is dedicated to my parents,
my nana and my sister.*

CONTENTS

ACKNOWLEDGEMENTS

First and foremost, I'd like to thank everyone who supported me during the research and writing process, including my parents, my sister, my nana, my cousin David, my fellow USC students and my brothers in Theta Chi fraternity—without your constant enthusiasm and encouragement, this book never would have been possible.

I'd also like to thank everyone who helped provide material for my research, including (but not limited to) Aisling Farrell, Richard Wojcik, the USC Libraries and the Los Angeles Public Library.

INTRODUCTION

When I entered USC as a freshman student in the fall of 2011, I knew next to nothing about the history of the school. On tours for prospective students, guides were always quick to point out Widney Alumni House, the oldest building on campus, but beyond that, little of the university's past was presented.

Given that I am an avid student of history, I quickly decided that, since I would be spending my next four years here, I would try to learn as much as possible about the history of the school and surrounding area. Soon, I found myself in the depths of USC's libraries or tracking down out-of-the-way historic markers on a daily basis. I gathered together as many historic photographs, maps, postcards, movies—essentially anything I could find that helped piece together the history of my school.

The first thing that struck me during my research was how much of USC's history has been preserved. This is, in large part, due to the fact that the campus expanded outward as it developed, so there was little need to replace preexisting buildings. With the exception of only a handful of buildings, nearly every major structure to be constructed on campus still stands, which is something few other schools in Southern California can claim.

I also noticed that it was impossible to solely focus on the history of USC without also looking at the surrounding areas. A USC professor founded Exposition Park to the south of campus. The North University Park neighborhood was developed because of an influx of wealthy citizens after the founding of the university. The story of USC is the story of University

Park in general, showing how a neighborhood and an educational institution can develop hand-in-hand.

As I continued my research, I began to view the campus in an entirely new way. Buildings I had once taken for granted were now impressive to me because I knew the stories behind the architects who designed them. Street corners that were formerly indistinguishable developed a whole new life in my eyes when I knew that Buster Keaton had filmed a movie there in the 1920s.

The spark that made me want to turn my casual research into a book was the excitement my fellow students showed when I shared with them what I had learned. No one knew that the original *King Kong* had been shot at the Shrine Auditorium. Or that Mickey Mantle had hit two home runs on campus against USC's baseball team. No one knew that THX audio was invented on campus. But whenever I'd tell one of my friends an interesting bit of trivia, they were fascinated.

I want this book to take readers on the same journey of discovery that I experienced in researching this history of my campus. Whether you're an alumnus, student, Trojan fan or fan of history in general, I like to think that there is something in this book for everybody. While it is by no means comprehensive, I have strived to make this book a solid starting point for delving into the history of one of the most significant neighborhoods in Los Angeles.

I've enjoyed learning as much as possible about University Park, and I hope you do, too. Thank you for joining me on this journey.

Chapter 1

THE EARLY HISTORY OF USC

1880–1921

THE FOUNDING OF USC

The idea of founding a university in Los Angeles can be traced back to at least 1871, when Judge Robert Maclay Widney began searching for suitable land for such an institution. Having been founded in 1781, Los Angeles was quickly being transformed from a sleepy Spanish village of a few hundred people into one of the largest cities on the West Coast. The arrival of the Southern Pacific Railroad and the discovery of oil helped to expedite this growth in the later decades of the nineteenth century. Widney, who had moved to California in 1857, felt that despite the "wild-west" nature of Los Angeles, there was still hope for an institute of higher education to be established in the city.

Initially, local landowner and Southern California pioneer Abel Stearns was interested in donating land for such a place. However, his death in 1871 forced Widney to look to other sources. Unfortunately, the Panic of 1873 quickly halted Widney's plans to establish a university, and a drought in 1877 further destroyed economic growth in the region. However, in the midst of this, a prominent Methodist elder, Reverend John R. Tansey, expressed interest and even donated land in order to fund a university; he died shortly thereafter, though, and progress was once again stopped.

However, once the depression had subsided by 1879, Judge Widney again began to map out plans for the university. In May 1879, Widney met with three men: Dr. Joseph P. Widney (brother of Judge Robert Widney), E.F.

Robert Maclay Widney, founder of the University of Southern California. Born in Ohio, Widney was a judge and a lawyer when he moved to Los Angeles in 1867. In 1879, Widney selected the university's first board of trustees and secured 308 acres of land from Ozro W. Childs, Isaias W. Hellman and John G. Downey. Widney's younger brother, Joseph Pomeroy Widney, would go on to be USC's second president.

Spence and A.M. Hough, to decide on questions such as where the university should be located and where to find funding.

Approximately 308 acres of land for the university was donated by three prominent Los Angeles citizens: Ozro W. Childs, John G. Downey and Isaias W. Hellman. These three men came from different religious backgrounds (Protestant, Catholic and Jewish, respectively), but all felt strongly about the need for an institution of higher learning in Los Angeles. Childs, who was born in Vermont and became a noted horticulturalist later in life, helped to construct the city's irrigation ditches and received a large parcel of land in return. Downey, an Irishman, helped found the Los Angeles Water Company and briefly served as the governor of California. Hellman, a Bavarian-born banker, helped establish Los Angeles's first synagogue before his involvement with USC.

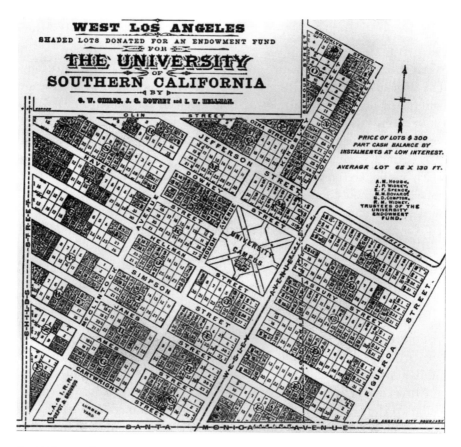

An 1880 map of University Park, showing the location of USC's first building and the lots that were sold to raise money for the university. Almost all of the street names on the map have been changed. Interestingly, this map depicts the entirety of USC's present-day campus, showing how much the school has grown since its inception. *Photo courtesy of the University of Southern California archives.*

The land that had been donated by Reverend Tansey and his wife years prior was sold in fifty-dollar lots to raise money for the university; generous buyers, however, donated more than double that amount of money for the land. On July 29 of that year, the official trust deed for the University of Southern California was drawn up by Childs, Downey and Hellman. The first trustees of the university consisted of the four men who had met in May, along with G.B. Compton and Marion McKinley Bovard (who would go on to be the university's first president).

USC's First Building

When the university first started in 1880, it consisted of only one structure. The original university building was a two-story, wooden Italianate structure constructed on the original plot of land given to the university. Designed by architects E.F. Kysor and Octavius Morgan at a cost of only $5,060, the cornerstone was laid on September 4, 1880. Almost one-tenth of the population of Los Angeles attended the ceremony to see the partially completed building, which was finished on October 4 and opened its doors for classes two days later. Initially, the school consisted of only fifty-three students, and all classes—from science to literature to philosophy—were held in this one building.

Over the years, the original university building has served a number of purposes and has been moved three times around campus. The building first occupied the southern part of the original USC land grant, near where the Norton Cinema Theater is today. Once the university began to expand, the building changed hands a number of times, including being the home of civil engineering, chemistry and the School of Music. The first move came in 1929, when the building was relocated westward to the corner of Hellman Way and Watt Way, where the Annenberg School for Communication currently sits. The building remained here (as the School of Music) until December 1955, when it was moved to Childs Way, east of Hubbard Hall and south of Doheny Library. It was also at this time that the original university building (also called Widney Hall) became the first USC building to be declared a California State Historic Landmark, dedicating it as the oldest university building in all of Southern California.

In 1977, the building underwent a complete renovation, which included the removal of the 1890s additions, thus restoring the building to its original appearance. One last move took place in July 1997, to make way for Lewis Hall; the original building was moved slightly northeast to its current location near Marks Hall. Today, the building is known as the Widney Alumni House, serving as the headquarters of the USC Alumni Association.

Opposite, top: An early drawing of USC's first building, now known as the Widney Alumni House. Constructed between September 4 and October 4, 1880, the building cost only about $5,000. It was designed by E.F. Kysor and Octavius Morgan. In the university's earliest days, all classes were held in this one building. *Photo courtesy of the University of Southern California archives.*

Opposite, bottom: A modern view of USC's first building. After being moved three times, the building currently serves as the headquarters of the USC Alumni Association and is a California State Historic Landmark. In 1977, the structure was restored to its original 1880 appearance.

The Fledgling University

Within a year of the university being founded, housing was already an issue for students. In January 1881, Mr. and Mrs. William H. Hodge announced their plans to construct a dormitory for twenty-five students, which would be named Hodge Hall in their honor. William Hodge, a carpenter, constructed the building himself with help from fellow churchgoers. Although initially located off campus, it was quickly moved to the southwest corner of the original campus, where the Annenberg School currently is. A men's dormitory, Lothian Hall, was added the following year. In those first years, the university was incredibly strict, banning all tobacco, alcohol, gambling, cursing and even leaving campus without permission.

The first president of USC was a man by the name of Marion McKinley Bovard. Bovard, who was born on January 11, 1847, in Alpha, Indiana, attended De Pauw University before traveling west for missionary work. Judge Tansey, who had first donated land for a university, urged Bovard to consider becoming president of the newly founded USC. Eventually, on October 5, 1880, Bovard was inaugurated in one of the upper rooms of the original university building (now Widney Alumni House). The next day, classes would begin in the same building.

During Marion Bovard's eleven-year term, his brother, Freeman D. Bovard, served as vice-president. Within the next few months, Marion Bovard worked to establish a debate team and a university marching band, the latter of which would go on to become one of the most celebrated collegiate bands in the entire country. Other early accomplishments were the establishment of a Department of Music in 1884, as well as the founding of the Maclay School of Theology and the USC College of Medicine in 1885.

For the most part, the first seven years of USC's history were successful and prosperous. The student population rapidly increased, as did the number of faculty and professors. Institutions such as the USC libraries and the University Museum were established by Bovard within a few months, rapidly increasing the academic capacity of the newly founded university. The surrounding community also developed quickly, and by September 7, 1883, the cornerstone for the nearby University Church had been laid.

The year 1884 was a transformative one for USC. On June 15 of that year, the first graduation ceremony was held—for only three students. In preparation, the university designed its first seal to put on the diplomas. One of the original graduates was the younger brother of USC's president and vice-president, Mr. George Finley Bovard. The youngest Bovard would

An early view of USC's Old College building in the 1890s. Old College, which was constructed in 1884, was USC's first brick building. In addition to classrooms, Old College housed USC's first library and museum. *Photo courtesy of the University of Southern California archives.*

found the USC Alumni Association in 1895, as well going on to become USC's fourth president in 1903.

The year 1884 also saw the construction of the first of many brick buildings on USC's campus. The cornerstone for what came to be known as "Old College" was laid on September 20 of that year. Old College, which was completed on January 9, 1887, was the first truly collegiate-looking building on USC's campus. Housing primarily the College of Liberal Arts, the building was built in a Classical revival style and featured a 116-foot clock tower, science laboratories in the basement, a five-hundred-seat chapel, offices and classrooms, all at a cost of $37,000. It was situated to the north of the original university building alongside University Avenue (now Trousdale Parkway).

In 1905, large extensions were added to both the north and south, increasing the amount of classroom and office space available at the school. Old College managed to survive for sixty years before succumbing to progress in 1948; the building was demolished to make way for Founders (now Taper) Hall. By the time it was torn down, Old College was showing many signs of wear and is today all but forgotten at USC.

By 1887, USC's prosperity was beginning to dwindle due to a widespread financial crisis in California, and the school entered a period of fiscal

A later view of the Old College building, showing the large wings that were added in 1905. Located on the site of today's Taper Hall, Old College was one of the most iconic buildings on USC's campus for the first half of the twentieth century. Finally, time took its toll on the building, and it was demolished in 1948. *Photo courtesy of the University of Southern California archives.*

uncertainty. One of the highlights of Bovard's later years, however, was the establishment of a USC football team, which would play its first game in 1888. However, overall enrollment decreased dramatically, and the university struggled to keep faculty members employed. Unfortunately, Marion Bovard died in December 1891, having led USC through its first eleven years. Bovard's achievements cannot be overstated; without his expert guidance and vision for the school, USC might not have survived its infancy and gone on to become the establishment it is today.

On January 11, 1892, the month after Bovard's death, Joseph Pomeroy Widney (one of USC's founding trustees) was elected to be USC's second president. Widney had been involved with the university from its earliest days, serving as the chair of literature and physiology before founding USC's medical school in 1885. Taking office, Widney faced the many challenges that

18

plagued Bovard's later years in office. Doing everything he could to reduce the school's debt, he took no salary while in office and rigorously increased the academic standards. It was under Widney that the university's first newspaper, the *Rostrum*, was published in 1892 (the current paper, the *Daily Trojan*, would first be published in 1912). The College of Music was founded in 1893.

Widney served as USC's president for three years before stepping down in 1895. In his brief time in office, he made great strides toward bringing USC out of debt and reestablishing the university as a major academic force. He also resigned from his position as the dean of the School of Medicine in 1896. He died on July 4, 1938, at the age of ninety-six, after a prolific life as a doctor, theologian, philosopher, author and activist.

USC's third president was an Episcopalian minister by the name of George Washington White. White had served on USC's board since 1890 and became chairman of the board three years later. By the time Widney resigned in September 1895, White was a natural choice to be elected president. Like his predecessor, White was faced with a large amount of debt, which he immediately began to tackle by soliciting donations from fellow churchgoers.

While president Widney had made great strides to promote the growth of the sciences on campus, White also encouraged the development of athletic programs. However, White also worked to modernize USC's science laboratories and acquire new volumes for the library. Enrollment hit a milestone five hundred people under White's administration. With conditions seemingly improving, White resigned in September 1899, after just four years in office.

Undoubtedly one of the most important achievements of this period was the adoption of cardinal and gold as USC's official school colors in 1895. Prior to this, each individual school within the university had its own colors. In 1958, the official gold was changed from an orange color to the yellow that it is today. The colors, which are officially called "USC Cardinal" and "USC Gold" (Pantone colors 201C and 123C, respectively), are registered trademarks of the university.

PRESIDENT GEORGE FINLEY BOVARD

For the four years following White's resignation, USC remained without a president. Each individual college was managed by its respective dean. Major executive decisions were made by the president of the board of trustees—

George Finley Bovard, younger brother of former president Marion Bovard and a member of USC's first graduating class in 1884. After four years of exemplary service to the university, Bovard was unanimously elected to the official position of president of USC on April 8, 1903. Bovard and his wife, Emma, soon moved to 801 West Thirty-fourth Street—a building that is still standing and is currently used as the offices for USC's Joint Educational Project.

Under president George Bovard, a physically imposing man who stood six-foot-four, USC began to resemble the university that exists today. In the years before World War I, the university saw a sharp increase in both enrollment and the scope of programs offered. In 1905, USC's School of Pharmacy was founded, offering a two-year graduate degree in the field. Other disciplines rapidly began popping up: in 1906, the first engineering classes were offered; in 1909, a Department of Education was established; and in 1912, USC became the first school in the world to offer a course on automobiles. By 1916, USC was the second-largest denominational college in the nation, well on its way to becoming a major institution of learning.

It was also during the Bovard years that two very unique students attended USC. The first, in 1915, was a ten-year-old girl by the name of Teresa Van Grove. Van Grove, who is still the youngest person ever to enroll at USC, was an extremely talented dancer who had dreams of being the "second Sarah Bernhardt." After spending a year studying dramatic arts at USC, she traveled to New York for an interview, but her eventual fate has been lost to time.

At the opposite end of the spectrum was Amy Winship, who was eighty-seven when she enrolled at USC in 1918. A childhood friend of Abraham Lincoln, Mrs. Winship decided at the age of seventy-nine to attend college for the first time in her life. After brief stints at the University of Wisconsin and the University of Ohio, she dedicated the rest of her life to traveling around the United States and studying the teaching methods of different universities, which eventually brought her to Southern California in 1918.

By the middle of the 1910s, everything seemed to be heading in the right direction for USC. Facilities were expanding, enrollment was increasing steadily and the curriculum was becoming more diverse. However, all of that changed when the United States entered World War I in 1917. Many students enrolled to serve overseas, and those who stayed behind began taking military training courses in place of regular physical education. The Student Army Training Corps established itself on campus shortly after the war began, and barracks and a YMCA headquarters were constructed along the western side of University Avenue (Trousdale Parkway). On October 1, 1918, almost one thousand students were inducted into the Student Army

Training Corps. Female students even knitted socks and sweaters for soldiers overseas as part of their classes.

At the end of the war, USC picked up right where it had left off. In 1919, just months after the armistice, the university established Southern California's first Architectural Department (individual classes having been taught since 1914). The department, which would become an independent school within the university in 1925, is currently ranked as one of the top architectural programs in the nation.

Bovard Administration Building

The year 1919 also saw the construction of arguably the most iconic and identifiable building at USC: George Finley Bovard Administration Building. Talk began in September 1919 about plans for a new, $500,000 building at the university that would be one of the crown jewels of Los Angeles (the final price tag ended up being $620,000). The job of designing such was given to noted Los Angeles architect John B. Parkinson, who would go on to design most of USC's landmark buildings. Parkinson, known for a wide range of architectural styles, went with a Northern Italian Renaissance revival design featuring intricate brickwork and a 116-foot clock tower. Ground was broken on October 14 by President Bovard himself (the building's namesake), and a cornerstone was provided as a gift from the senior class. Also present that day was USC co-founder Robert Maclay Widney, for whom the first university building was named.

It was decided early on that there were to be eight statues on top of the new building, symbolizing different tenants of the university and the "progress of civilization." The larger-than-life figures, sculpted by Johan Caspar Lachne Gruenfeld, span multiple millennia. On the main façade, facing east, are John Wesley, the founder of Methodism, and Matthew Simpson, a Methodist bishop, professor and the first president of Indiana Asbury (later DePauw) University. Both of these men represent the blending of religion and academia, as well as the Methodist affiliation of USC until 1952.

On the southern side of the building, facing the student union, are Phillips Brooke and Borden Parker Bowne. These men both symbolize America's role in theology and philosophy in the nineteenth century: Brooks was the Episcopalian bishop of Boston (and the author of the popular Christmas carol, "O Little Town of Bethlehem"), while Bowne was a noted author, theologian and philosophy professor at Boston University. Continuing to the west side of

Bovard Administration Building are the oldest figures represented: Roman orator and philosopher Marcus Tullius Cicero on the left and distinguished Greek philosopher Plato on the right. The remaining two statues, on the north side of the building, are two of the most important presidents in United States history: Abraham Lincoln and Theodore Roosevelt.

Bovard Administration Building was a major expansion for the university, as it was only the second brick building to be built after Old College. The centerpiece of the new building was the 1,235-seat auditorium, located directly inside the main entrance. When the venue opened, it featured a $35,000 pipe organ designed by the Robert Morton Company. The organ was removed in the 1970s and was dispersed; part of it was incorporated into the Crystal Cathedral (now Christ Cathedral) in Orange, California.

In addition to the auditorium, the building also included administrative offices for the university, as well as twenty-seven classrooms. The north wing of the building housed the James Harmon Hoose Hall of Philosophy, and the south wing housed the Thomas Blanchard Stowell Hall of Education. Hoose, for whom the philosophy wing was named, was a prolific professor in the early days of the university—it was because of Hoose that philosophy, history, sociology, economics and psychology programs were developed at USC. Stowell, the namesake of the education wing, was the head of the Education Department for many years, as well as being a respected neurologist, anatomist, historian and psychologist.

Bovard Administration Building was opened after more than a year and a half of construction on June 19, 1921. A baccalaureate sermon was given by Methodist bishop Adna Wright Leonard. However, the day was bittersweet for many people, as it marked the end of George Finley Bovard's term as president. Health issues had begun to take their toll, and he was advised by his doctors to resign from his post. There is no more fitting tribute, however, for such a leader than a building as grand as Bovard Hall.

Opposite, top: A circa 1920 aerial view of USC's campus, showing Old College with the Bovard Administration Building under construction directly below it. To the left of Old College can be seen Widney Hall, USC's first building. Also visible is USC's football field, Bovard Field, as well as an early gymnasium, chemistry building and the Hodge Hall dormitory. *Photo courtesy of the University of Southern California archives.*

Opposite, bottom: George Finley Bovard Administration Building and Auditorium, shortly after its completion in 1921. This is currently USC's oldest brick building. This photo was taken long before University Avenue (now Trousdale Parkway) was closed to traffic, and trolley tracks can be seen running along the street. Constructed at a cost of $620,000, the building was named after USC's fourth president. *Photo courtesy of the University of Southern California archives.*

Today, many traces of the early days of the university have been destroyed. The site of the original gymnasium is now where the Bing Theater sits. The location of the former chemistry and pharmacy "shack" is now the home of the Annenberg School for Communication. Two of the original science buildings, the engineering and geology buildings, were replaced by Zumberge Hall and the Law School building, respectively. The original student union building and bookstore has been replaced. However, fortunately the Widney Alumni House still stands as an ever-present reminder of the university's earliest days and the men who devoted so much of their lives to bringing higher education to Los Angeles.

Chapter 2

THE RISE OF USC

1921–1957

PRESIDENT RUFUS B. VON KLEINSMID

President George F. Bovard's resignation in 1921 represented the end of the first chapter of USC's history. However, the next chapter would prove to be even grander for the still-developing university. USC's fifth president would be Rufus Bernhard von KleinSmid. Dr. Von, as he affectionately became known to his students, was born in Sandwich, Illinois, in 1875. He received his bachelor's, master's and doctorate degrees from Northwestern University and was a professor of education and psychology at DePauw University shortly thereafter.

In 1914, von KleinSmid became the seventh president of the University of Arizona, a position he would hold for seven years before becoming president of USC. He accepted the offer to come to Los Angeles on October 10, 1921, and was inaugurated on April 28 of the following year. When he began at USC, the university consisted of only eight schools and fewer than six thousand students; within less than a decade, the school had over fifteen thousand students enrolled.

Many notable occurrences happened during von KleinSmid's time in office. The year he was inaugurated, a student by the name of Milo Sweet composed "Fight On," USC's official fight song, as part of a contest. In 1924, von KleinSmid established the first school of international relations in the nation; the following year, he would establish a school of engineering. Academic offerings continued to expand; in 1927, the first PhD from USC

A portrait of Rufus B. von KleinSmid, USC's fifth president from 1921 to 1947. Under von KleinSmid, many of USC's most iconic buildings were constructed, and the university began to rise in national prominence. During his later years, he served as the chancellor of USC until his death in 1964. *Photo courtesy of the Los Angeles Public Library.*

was conferred, and in 1929 the School of Public Administration and the Department of Cinema were founded.

THE 1920S: A DECADE OF CONSTRUCTION

Von KleinSmid quickly set out to expand the university physically as well as academically. One of the first buildings constructed under President von KleinSmid was the Stoops Library. Designed by Hibbard, Gerity and Kerton, the Stoops Library was constructed as the University Branch of the Los Angeles Public Library during a time when new branch libraries were being constructed across the city. The building, which cost $66,444 to construct, formally opened on September 25, 1923, with a ceremony that featured von KleinSmid himself.

When the building was constructed, it faced due west on University Avenue (directly across from the JEP House). However, when Hoover Street was constructed in 1931, the building had to be moved back and placed at an angle, as it currently sits. For the first ten years of its existence, the Stoops Library was the primary library that served students; however, the construction of Doheny Library in 1932 significantly reduced its usage. USC acquired the building in 1965, at which point it became the home of the school's Education Library. In May 1999, it reopened as the East Asian Library, and in 2011 it was once again repurposed and expanded, opening in 2012 as the new location of the University Club restaurant.

The year after the construction of Stoops Library saw further development in the construction of a Hall of Science. Located on the northwest corner of Thirty-seventh Street and University Avenue, it was located immediately south of USC's original engineering building. After designing Bovard Administration Building in 1919, John Parkinson (as well as his son, Donald Parkinson) began a long-term relationship with USC that resulted in the construction of many of USC's most iconic buildings.

When the Hall of Science was first constructed in 1924 (at a cost of $500,000), it consisted of a simple, Italian Romanesque–style U-shaped building occupying the southern half of the block. Designed specifically for the Chemistry and Pharmacy Departments, the four-story building featured state-of-the-art laboratories, scientific machinery and a library. Four years later, the Parkinsons would expand the Hall of Science north to Thirty-sixth Place, replacing the former engineering building. This addition, at a

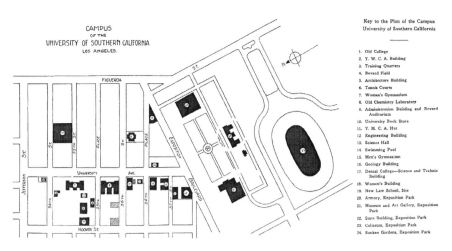

A 1925 map of USC's campus, showing the rapid development under President von KleinSmid. When von KleinSmid took office in 1921, USC consisted of only three blocks; by the time the map was drawn, it had more than doubled in size. By the start of the 1930s, University Avenue would be lined with impressive, Romanesque brick buildings.

USC's Science Hall, now known as Zumberge Hall. The southern half (left side of the photo) was constructed in 1924; the northern half was added four years later, in 1928. This is one of many buildings on USC's campus designed by the father-and-son architectural team of John and Donald Parkinson. The entryway of Zumberge Hall features a 1937 mural by a fine arts student. Today, the building houses USC's Department of Earth Sciences and Southern California Earthquake Center. *Photo courtesy of the Los Angeles Public Library.*

cost of $372,000, provided space for zoology, botany, optometry, physics and medicine. Today, everything south of the central arcade was built in 1924; the central section and northern wing are the 1928 addition. Despite being constructed in 1928, the building wasn't dedicated until June 1930.

In the center entranceway of the building is a tile mural titled *Science and Youth*. The mural was created in 1937 by Jean Goodwin Ames as a master's in fine arts project. Jean, alongside her husband, Arthur, would go on to paint many murals in Southern California as part of the Works Progress Administration. In 2003, the Hall of Science was renamed the Zumberge Hall of Science to honor former USC president James H. Zumberge. Today, the building is home to the Earth Sciences Department and the Southern California Earthquake Center.

Across from the Science Hall, another Parkinson and Parkinson–designed building was announced in 1924 and erected by 1926. Located on the site of the former geology building, the new USC Law School Building was constructed at a cost of $165,000. More than seventy different academic institutions were represented at the building's formal opening on February 5, 1926. The Italian Romanesque style of the building blends seamlessly with the surrounding buildings. Today, the former Law School Building is the Leventhal School of Accounting.

In 1924, plans were also announced for the construction of a women's dormitory. The building, located on Thirty-sixth Street, was finished by the middle of August 1925 and was opened to students at the start of the 1925 academic year. Featuring mahogany woodwork and a large central fireplace, the building, designed by William Lee Woollett, cost approximately $150,000. The funds were raised by a campaign led by Elisabeth von KleinSmid, the president's wife. The second and third floors were dedicated to four-person rooms for female students, with the bottom floor featuring dining halls and a kitchen. Beginning around 1935, the dormitory began being referred to as Elisabeth von KleinSmid Hall, as opposed to just the Women's Residence Hall.

Initially, plans called for a second dormitory building to be constructed immediately south fronting Thirty-sixth Place; however, these plans fell through, and in 1935 the Foyer of Town & Gown was constructed. This second building, which was designed by John and Donald Parkinson, cost $65,000 and was dedicated on October 25, 1935. It featured an outdoor patio, kitchen and enough space for seven hundred guests. A year later, the Little Chapel of Silence was added to the Foyer. The chapel, which was renovated in 1978, is still one of USC's hidden gems.

Town & Gown, the group for which the building was constructed, is the oldest women's organization at USC. Originally founded as the Women's Club of USC in 1904, the group has continued to provide student scholarships and campus building funds for over a century. Today, social events are still held in the Foyer of Town & Gown, while the Women's Residence Hall became the Student Academic Services Building before being renamed John Hubbard Hall (after USC's eighth president) in September 2003.

With a women's dormitory being constructed in 1925, it didn't take long for a men's dormitory to follow. In 1927, Aeneas Hall was constructed on Thirty-sixth Place to accommodate 155 male students. The name, celebrating the valiant Trojan warrior, was selected by President von KleinSmid himself. For a few short years during World War II, the building housed naval students and was renamed Newkirk Hall; the name was changed back to Aeneas Hall by 1949, but by the mid-1950s, it had become known as Stonier Hall. Stonier Hall served as a men's dormitory until the early 1970s; today, the building houses offices and the Spirit of Troy marching band.

Construction on a long-awaited student union began in June 1927. Located on the southwest corner of Thirty-sixth Street and University Avenue, the new building replaced the Associated Students' Store. The building, designed by Parkinson and Parkinson (like so many other buildings from this period), was the North Italian Renaissance style typical of USC but also featured many Gothic revival elements. Dozens of terra cotta figures were sculpted by Gladding, McBean & Co. depicting student life and activities; among the more infamous is a monkey thumbing his nose at President von KleinSmid, whom many of the builders found overbearing. The building cost $325,000 to construct; much of the financing was provided by the football team.

Opposite, top: A 1930s view looking west down Thirty-sixth Street. On the right is Bovard Administration Building, with the newly added *Trojan Shrine* sculpture in front. Behind Bovard Auditorium, the corner of the Physical Education Building (constructed in 1930) can be seen. On the left is USC's student union building, begun in 1927 and opened in 1928. The student union was funded in large part by USC's football team. *Photo courtesy of the University of Southern California archives.*

Opposite, bottom: Circa late 1930s photo looking north on University Avenue (now Trousdale Parkway). On the left side of the photo, the Hall of Science can be seen, followed by the student union building and Bovard Administration Building. On the right side of the street, Bridge Hall (1928) and the Law School Building (1926) can be seen. It should also be noted that the trolley cars along University Avenue had been removed by this time. *Photo courtesy of the University of Southern California archives.*

The building opened on March 3, 1928, with a banquet. The first floor contained the student store, barbershops and a coffee shop; the upper floors contained offices for the *Daily Trojan, El Rodeo* yearbook and other publications. There was also a Social Hall used for school dances that could accommodate five hundred people, as well as a central patio that has since been removed. Today, the building houses offices, a pharmacy and other student services.

In late 1927, it was announced that USC would continue its expansion with the construction of Bridge Hall. The four-story building, which would contain thirty-four classrooms and numerous offices, was dedicated to Dr. and Mrs. Norman Bridge, two benefactors of the university since 1892 who passed away in 1925. Located next to the Law School Building, Bridge Hall was also designed by John and Donald Parkinson in an Italian Romanesque style, making it blend seamlessly with other buildings from the era. Construction of the $208,000 Bridge Hall began on October 24, 1927, and was completed in March of the following year. Over the years, the building has served the Engineering Department; the College of Letters, Arts and Sciences; and, most recently, the Marshall School of Business.

USC Enters the 1930s

Construction did not slow down as the Roaring Twenties came to a close. On May 16, 1929, the cornerstone was laid for the Seeley Wintersmith Mudd Hall of Philosophy. Mudd, a U.S. Army colonel and noted mining engineer, and his family were donors for the construction of the new building. It is interesting to note that this is one of the few substantial buildings from this time not designed by the Parkinsons; instead, Ralph Carlin Flewelling created the unique blend of architectural styles, including Tuscan and Italian Romanesque. Dedicated on June 5, 1930, Mudd Hall cost $300,000 to construct.

Mudd Hall of Philosophy has come to be one of the most iconic buildings on USC's campus. Notable architectural features include a cloistered courtyard and a 146-foot bell tower; inside, one can find Argonauts' Hall (originally built for the philosophy club and now used as a classroom, it features a mural of Jason and the Argonauts) and Borden Parker Bowne Hall (named after the famed Methodist professor, who is also featured as one of the eight large statues on Bovard Auditorium). What were formerly a rare book room and

The Seeley Wintersmith Mudd Hall of Philosophy, constructed in 1930. One of USC's most iconic buildings, Mudd Hall contains the James Harmon Hoose Library of Philosophy. Designed by Ralph Carlin Flewelling, the building is a unique mix of Tuscan and Italian Romanesque architecture. *Photo courtesy of the University of Southern California archives.*

a book bindery are now classrooms and offices. Undoubtedly, the highlight of the building, though, is the James Harmon Hoose Library of Philosophy, located on the second story. Named after USC's first philosophy professor, the Hoose Library grew out of a small collection of books kept in the Old College building in the first years of the twentieth century. The main reading room features an impressive stone fireplace, stained-glass windows and twenty-two mosaics of famous philosophers throughout history. The adjacent Ralph Tyler Flewelling Reading Room was named after the president of the School of Philosophy when Mudd Hall was constructed.

In 1930, USC was also celebrating its fiftieth anniversary. The highlight of the festivities came on June 6, 1930, when the *Trojan Shrine* statue was unveiled. Now informally referred to by students as "Tommy Trojan," the design was sculpted by Roger Noble Burnham, who used USC football players such as Russ Saunders, Ernie Pinckert, Henry Becker, Larry Stevens and John Ward as reference. Constructed at a cost of $10,000, the statue was funded in part by adding a $1 surplus to football season tickets.

Arguably the most iconic monument on USC's campus, the front of the base of the *Trojan Shrine* features inscriptions of the five attributes of the ideal Trojan: Faithful, Scholarly, Skillful, Courageous and Ambitious. The back of the shrine features a quote from Virgil: "Here are provided seats of meditative joy, where shall arise again the destined reign of Troy."

USC's original men's gymnasium, which was located where the Fischer Museum of Art now stands, was destroyed by a tragic fire on the night of May 29, 1929. Immediately, the university began work on the new Physical Education Building. Designed by John and Donald Parkinson, the new building would feature men's and women's gymnasiums, locker rooms, handball courts, administrative offices and three swimming pools. Ground was broken on the new building on November 12, 1929, and the structure was completed just less than a year later, on October 6, 1930. A dedication ceremony was held at the homecoming dance on December 1 of that year. Today, the building houses ROTC offices, dance studios and kinesiology labs.

On May 24, 1931, the cornerstone was laid for the brand-new University Methodist Church. The festivities that day also celebrated the fiftieth anniversary of the founding of the church, which had formerly been located on the southwest corner of Jefferson Boulevard and McClintock Avenue. A time capsule that had been placed in the old church in 1883, along with a new time capsule from 1931, was placed in the cornerstone of the $180,000 structure. At the cornerstone-laying ceremony were the only three surviving charter members of the church, including the widow of USC's first president, Marion Bovard.

One of USC's most iconic buildings is Edward L. Doheny Jr. Memorial Library, which was dedicated on September 12, 1932. Doheny Jr. (also known as Ned) was the son of the oil magnate who owned the nearby Chester Place housing tract and a USC graduate, active alumnus and benefactor. On the evening of February 16, 1929, Ned was tragically and mysteriously murdered at his Beverly Hills home, the Greystone Mansion. The murderer was Doheny's secretary, Hugh Plunkett; however, details surrounding the murder and Plunkett's subsequent suicide are sketchy, and there are many prominent rumors regarding the incident.

What is certain, however, is that following Ned's death, Mr. and Mrs. Doheny Sr. funded the construction of the library in his memory. President von KleinSmid and the Doheny family selected architect Ralph Adams Cram to design the exterior of the building, while Samuel Eugene Lunden designed the interiors and refined Cram's plan. The cornerstone was laid on December 3, 1931. After only nine months of construction, the building was completed.

Architecturally, Doheny Memorial Library is one of the more (if not the most) significant buildings on USC's campus. Externally, the building is a unique blend of Mediterranean and Romanesque architecture, managing to blend into the surrounding buildings while still emerging as the highlight of campus. An

Edward L. Doheny Jr. Memorial Library under construction in 1932. Named in honor of the son of Los Angeles oil magnate Edward Doheny, the library features nine floors of books, as well as lavish sculptures, murals, woodwork and stained glass throughout, making it one of USC's most impressive buildings. *Photo courtesy of the University of Southern California archives.*

entire team of sculptors, muralists and other artists were employed to decorate the lavish interior. Highlights include extensive stained glass depicting scholars throughout history, sculptures of Dante and Shakespeare on the building's façade and intricate murals and woodwork throughout the building.

The highlight of the building is the Main Reading Room (now called the Los Angeles Times Reference Room), stretching 131 by 46 feet with a two-and-a-half-story-high ceiling. Also on the first floor are the Treasure Room (now used for rotating exhibits), the Current Periodicals Reading Room, the East Asian Library and the former card catalogue room. Below, the ground floor of the building contains the Cinema-Television Library, the David L. Wolper Center and the Music Library. The building's second floor contains offices and additional collections, as well as the Horton Rare Book Room. A majority of Doheny Library's books, however, are held in the building's stacks area, which contains a remarkable nine stories of books.

The Late 1930s and World War II

The late 1930s saw the construction of the few buildings on USC's campus that could be considered Art Deco in style. One that is often forgotten is Biegler Hall of Engineering (originally just called the Engineering Building), which was constructed at a cost of $86,000 (with equipment, the cost totaled $175,000) by the fall of 1940. The building was dedicated at a ceremony with President von KleinSmid on December 4, 1940. At the time, there were only 385 engineering students at USC; today, there are over 5,300. Designed by C. Raimond Johnson alongside John and Donald Parkinson, Biegler Hall features fluted pilasters that are reminiscent of what has been deemed the "Greco Deco" style of architecture.

Another building from this time is the May Ormerad Harris Hall for the College of Architecture and Fine Arts. Completed by September 9, the building was opened for classes on September 18, 1939. A more formal dedication was held between January 18 and 20 the following year; amongst the guest speakers that weekend was famed architect Frank Lloyd Wright. Ralph C. Flewelling, who also designed Mudd Hall of Philosophy next door, designed Harris Hall in the Streamline Moderne style of Art Deco that was popular at the time. Located within the building is the USC Fisher Museum of Art, named after art collector and USC benefactor Elizabeth Holmes Fisher. The museum currently holds about 1,800 pieces of art, with exhibits frequently being interchanged.

One of the most important names in the development of USC as a major research institute is George Allan Hancock. Born on July 26, 1875, in San Francisco, Hancock inherited the 4,439-acre Mexican land grant known as Rancho La Brea from his father. Hancock worked to develop the land, which would become neighborhoods such as Hancock Park, Fairfax and the Miracle Mile. A man of many talents, Hancock was an avid naturalist and frequently took voyages on his ship, the *Velero III*, to collect specimens for different institutions.

On New Year's Day 1938, it was announced that an Allan Hancock Foundation for Scientific Research would be founded at USC. Plans were quickly made for the construction of a building to provide facilities for zoological and botanical research. Ground was broken on January 5 of the following year at a very prominent site in the heart of campus. Designed by C. Raimond Johnson with consultation from Samuel E. Lunden, the building is perhaps the best example of Art Deco architecture at USC, while still managing to blend seamlessly with the

The George Allan Hancock Foundation Building, constructed between 1939 and 1941. Covered in relief sculptures depicting various assets of natural history, the building is arguably the best example of late Art Deco architecture on USC's campus. The Hancock Foundation Building also features four original rooms from Hancock's 1913 mansion, preserved as a museum.

surrounding buildings. Small relief panels along the top of the building depict the evolution of animal life over time, as well as species that were collected by Hancock's *Velero III* on its many voyages. Larger relief sculptures on the north and east sides of the building depict animals discovered at the La Brea Tar Pits, which Hancock donated to the City of Los Angeles. The total cost of the building, which was dedicated on January 3 and 4, 1941, was over $660,000.

Inside, the Hancock Foundation Building was just as impressive as it was on the outside. More than one hundred labs were included for scientific research, as well as six levels of fireproof storage for specimens. Also included were a scientific library, greenhouse and telescope. Hancock, in addition to being a naturalist, was also passionate about music. An accomplished cellist himself (he often played with the Los Angeles Symphony Orchestra), he included two auditoriums in the building, one of which was renovated in 1999 and reopened as the Alfred Newman Recital Hall.

The highlight of the Hancock Foundation Building, however, are the four rooms that were preserved from the Hancock family mansion, which was built on the northeast corner of Wilshire Boulevard and Vermont Avenue in 1913. When the house was slated for demolition, Hancock had four rooms—

the reception hall, dining room, library and music salon—transported down Vermont Avenue on specially designed dollies. Today, the four rooms are contained in the southeast wing of the Hancock Foundation Building, serving as a museum and memorial to Hancock's mother.

THE POSTWAR YEARS

Following World War II, construction started up again on campus. The Old College building, dating back to 1884, was demolished in 1948 after being deemed a fire and earthquake hazard. Work quickly began on a replacement, which came in the form of the $1 million Founders Hall, designed by the architectural team of Marsh, Smith and Powell. When it opened on May 15, 1950, its capacity of 2,700 students was double the number that Old College could accommodate. In April 1980, a $4.8 million renovation and addition was begun, including a twenty-six-thousand-square-foot addition to the south side of the building. The two-year project was completed in May 1982, at which point the building was renamed Taper Hall of Humanities after USC benefactor Mark Taper.

The post–World War II period also saw the inauguration of USC's sixth president, Fred Dow Fagg Jr. A graduate of the University of Redlands and Northwestern University, he went on to teach at Northwestern, in addition to being the dean of its Kellogg School of Management and vice-president of the university. His inauguration took place on September 8, 1947, with von KleinSmid becoming the chancellor.

In April 1948, Fagg dedicated twenty-nine buildings on the university's campus, which had been relocated from Santa Ana Air Base after the war. He also oversaw the purchase of large tracts of land, expanding USC's campus until it began to resemble the footprint it has today. While von KleinSmid's presidency was characterized by extensive spending and construction, Fagg's presidency was much more focused on increasing the scope of USC's academic programs and solidifying the university as a prominent institution of higher education.

Numerous other buildings were constructed during the years after World War II. At some point prior to 1948, the building located on the southeast corner of Jefferson Boulevard and McClintock Avenue was constructed for the Los Angeles College of Optometry, established downtown in 1904. In 1968, plans for a new building near the same site were announced, but four years later the college moved to its present location in Fullerton, California. The old optometry building is currently used by the USC College of Letters, Arts and Sciences.

Amongst the smaller buildings built during this period are the Student Health Center and the YWCA building. Designed in 1950 by Gordon B. Kaufman and J.E. Stanton, the Claire Zellerback Saroni Student Health Center served USC's students until the end of 2012, when the new Engemann Health Center opened a few blocks away. The following year, the Belle D. Vivian YWCA Building was designed by Vincent Palmer & Associates; this building was demolished in 2012 to make way for the future Wallis Annenberg Hall. Also constructed were the Commons, built in 1950 and later replaced by the Ronald Tutor Campus Center, and the Harold E. and Lillian M. Moulton Organic Chemistry Wing, completed in 1951.

Prior to 1952, the USC School of Dentistry had been housed in a triangular building on the corner of Exposition Boulevard and Thirty-sixth Place (near the site of the current law school building). In 1952, a significantly larger building was constructed on the northern part of campus. Upgraded by J.E. Stanton and William F. Stockwell in 1969, the $4 million structure was one of the most high-tech facilities of its kind when constructed. The former dental school building was ultimately demolished in the early 1970s.

During this period of USC's history, there were also several local buildings that were acquired by USC and used as housing for students. In addition to several apartments along Jefferson Boulevard, the two most prominent were Touton Hall and Harris Plaza. Touton Hall, located near the intersection of McClintock Avenue and Thirty-fourth Street, was an apartment building constructed in the 1920s and purchased by USC in 1955. At the other end of campus, just south of Harris Hall, was Harris Plaza. Originally constructed as housing for athletes in the 1932 Olympics, it later became housing for both men and women at USC. Both buildings were closed at the end of the spring 1986 semester due to concerns regarding earthquake safety, despite attempts to save the buildings due to their historic natures.

Chapter 3

THE MODERNIZATION OF USC

1957–PRESENT

RECENT PRESIDENTS OF THE UNIVERSITY

Norman H. Topping was inaugurated as USC's seventh president on October 23, 1958, in front of a crowd of 1,800 in Bovard Auditorium. Born in Flat River, Missouri, Topping was a USC graduate himself, receiving his bachelor's degree in 1933 and his MD in 1936, and went on to work for the U.S. Public Health Service during World War II. From 1952 to 1958, he was the vice-president for medical affairs at the University of Pennsylvania; he was selected as USC's president from a field of more than two hundred candidates.

The Topping years were among the most prosperous in USC's history. Topping announced his "Master Plan for Enterprise and Excellence in Education" in May 1961, calling for over $106 million to be raised in two decades; the goal was met in almost one-fourth of that time. Further success came in 1969, when USC became one of forty-eight universities in the United States and Canada that are members of the Association of American Universities, which has been described as "the pre-eminent research-intensive membership group" for universities.

Topping announced his resignation on April 27, 1970, due to minor health ailments. He continued to serve the university for the rest of his life, however, serving as chancellor from 1971 to 1980 and being appointed emeritus chancellor in 1980. He passed away after a bout with pneumonia on November 18, 1997, at the age of eighty-nine.

John Randolph Hubbard was born in 1918 in Belton, Texas. He attended the University of Texas and earned his PhD in 1950, studying history. After a stint in the U.S. Navy, Hubbard lived in India for four years, serving as an adviser for the U.S. Agency for International Development. Hubbard's involvement with USC began in 1969, when he was appointed to the position of vice-president and provost. The following year, he was unanimously elected to become USC's eighth president.

Under Hubbard, USC continued to grow as a research institute, rising from Thirty-third to Nineteenth in National Science Foundation rankings. The sheer number of applications to attend USC also increased during his decade in office; by the end of the 1970s, nearly three times as many students were applying than when Hubbard took office.

From a fundraising standpoint, Hubbard was one of USC's most successful leaders. Launched in 1975, the "Toward Century II" campaign was designed to prepare USC for its second century. By the time USC celebrated its 100th birthday in 1980, $309 million had been raised. Following his retirement in 1980, he continued to hold the John R. Hubbard Chair in History and teach undergraduate courses in the history department. In September 2003, the Student Academic Services Building was renamed John R. Hubbard Hall; Hubbard passed away eight years later, on August 21, 2011.

Hubbard was succeeded by James Herbert Zumberge, a Minnesota native who had previously served as the president of Southern Methodist University. A noted geologist and Antarctic explorer, Zumberge managed to raise $641 million and construct twenty new buildings during his decade in office, while at the same time bringing a new reputability to the university. Both the National Center for Integrated Photonic Technology and the Southern California Earthquake Center were founded during his term. Shortly after his retirement on March 31, 1991, he was found to have a brain tumor, and he passed away a little more than a year later, on April 16, 1992. On November 11, 2003, USC's Hall of Science was rededicated Zumberge Hall.

Steven Browning Sample took over for Zumberge in March 1991. Holding the position until August 3, 2010, Sample continued to further USC's reputation as a research institute, as well as improving the university's communications program and increasing community outreach. USC's eleventh and current president (at the time of writing), C.L. Max Nikias, has served since August 2010. Like his predecessor Sample, Nikias's background is in electrical engineering. In the early years of his presidency, Nikias has continued to improve USC's academic offerings, research capabilities and on-campus facilities, overseeing the construction of many new buildings.

The Sciences at USC

In 1961, architect William L. Pereira, a Chicago native who worked out of Los Angeles, was hired to draw up Topping's master plan for USC's campus. Pereira, who designed such buildings as Los Angeles International Airport's Theme Building, the Los Angeles County Museum of Art and the original Disneyland Hotel, was noted for his futuristic designs, which grew out of his love of science fiction. Many of USC's buildings over the next few decades would be designed by his firm, Pereira & Associates.

The first major building to be built under Pereira's 1961 master plan was Olin Hall of Engineering. Construction for the complex began in February 1962 with a $2.2 million grant from the Olin Foundation. Olin Hall is actually a collection of five separate buildings—two five-story buildings containing classrooms, offices and laboratories, while another five-story building contains an elevator and stairwell. The complex is completed by two one-story buildings that were built to house an auditorium and a library. All five buildings are connected by open-air bridges and platforms. Pereira's architecture is very typical of his Midcentury Modern style, which he would revisit with later buildings on USC's campus. The complex was dedicated on September 25, 1963.

USC's science facilities grew greatly in the mid-1960s. On April 27, 1964, the Ahmanson Center for Biological Research was dedicated, a three-building, $2 million complex financed by USC alumnus Howard Ahmanson and the National Institute of Health. Two of the buildings are five-story laboratory structures, containing eighty laboratories and twenty offices for 250 scientists. The third building is a seven-story tower designed to house up to seven thousand animals for research purposes; all three buildings are connected by a series of bridges. Designed by William Pereira & Associates, the buildings' hooded windows have led to their affectionately being referred to as the "cheese-grater buildings."

In December 1964, only months after the Ahmanson Center was completed, construction began on another building adjacent to the three already built. The Stauffer Chemical Company donated a tract of land in San Luis Obispo to the university, valued at $400,000; USC put the profits toward the new $1 million science hall. Named the Stauffer Hall of Science, it is identical in design to the Ahmanson Center's two laboratory towers. At the same time, the two-story, $300,000 John Stauffer Science Lecture Hall was being completed nearby, also designed by William Pereira. Both buildings were dedicated on October 5, 1966.

Students outside the Olin Hall of Engineering, a five-building complex constructed between 1962 and 1963. This was the first large science building to be completed under architect William L. Pereira's 1961 master plan for the university. *Photo courtesy of the University of Southern California archives.*

Coinciding with the construction of the Ahmanson Center and Stauffer Hall, a $232,000 addition to the Organic Chemistry Wing was constructed. Named the Laird J. Stabler Memorial Laboratories, the complex, which was dedicated on February 25, 1964, was constructed to conduct research on air quality. Stabler Hall is bordered on the east by the Robert Glen Rapp Engineering Research Building, which opened as the Nuclear Physics Laboratory in May 1958. Designed by Smith, Powell and Morgridge at a cost of $175,000, the building originally housed a $2 million, 32,000,000-electron-volt proton accelerator donated to USC by the Atomic Energy Commission.

The next major scientific building to be constructed at USC, Vivian Hall of Engineering, was dedicated on January 5, 1967. The seven-story building, named for Robert E. Vivian, former dean of the engineering school, cost $2.7 million. The lawn between Olin Hall and Vivian Hall came to be known as Archimedes Plaza by the early 1970s.

Left: One of the Ahmanson Center for Biological Research towers, completed in 1964. Along with the identical Stauffer Hall of Science, which was dedicated in 1966, these buildings helped to improve USC's Biology Department by providing laboratory space and housing for animals.

Below: Vivian Hall of Engineering, constructed in 1967, is one of the many science buildings from this era designed by noted Modernist architect William L. Pereira. The area between Vivian Hall and Olin Hall has come to be known as Archimedes Plaza.

Only three years after Vivian Hall was erected, USC opened the largest scientific complex on the West Coast at the time. The donor who financed the $4.8 million buildings was Mrs. Frank R. Seaver, wife of the late lawyer and industrialist who lived nearby on Chester Place before his death in 1964. The dedication, on January 22, 1970, featured a speech by Neil Armstrong. Today, the Seaver Science Center features seven stories of classrooms, offices and laboratories, while the adjoined Seaver Science Library houses more than thirty thousand books and journals.

Nearby, the Seaver Science Center is one of the first buildings built under President Hubbard. Charles Lee Powell Hall was dedicated on September 28, 1973. The $1.5 million, six-story building was named after the early Los Angeles engineer who is credited with building much of the city's infrastructure. Nearby, the Henry Salvatori Computer Science Center was opened in early 1976, further expanding the university's scientific capacity. The $2 million building was a direct response to the increasing number of students utilizing computers for their research.

Following the Salvatori Computer Science Center, William Pereira & Associates would go on to design only one more building on USC's campus: the Donald P. and Katherine B. Loker Hydrocarbon Institute. The $2 million complex opened on December 9, 1979, and was the first university-based center for hydrocarbon research in the world.

Many other, smaller science buildings were also constructed during this period. Construction of the Corwin D. Denney Research Center began in July 1978, and the building was completed by December of that year. Named after a Beverly Hills industrialist who donated $1 million of its $3.7 million cost, it was designed by William Allen & Associates. Four years later, the university built the Hedco Petroleum & Chemical Engineering Building, which was designed by longtime USC architect Samuel E. Lunden, who had designed Doheny Library more than half a century earlier (amongst numerous other buildings on campus). The $1.2 million, three-story building opened in May 1982.

At this same time, however, a much larger and more impressive building was being built nearby. Plans for the Seeley G. Mudd Building began as early as October 1977, when a $5 million grant from the Seeley G. Mudd Fund was made to USC. Construction of the $14.7 million, ten-story building, though, would not begin until early 1980. After more than three years, the building, which was designed by the architectural firm of Grillias, Pirc, Rosier & Alves, was finally dedicated on April 7, 1983. The building was designed specifically for the undergraduate chemistry and psychology programs, in addition to numerous other classrooms and offices. The Seeley G. Mudd Building is perhaps most notable as the tallest functional building on USC's campus; at 167 feet, it stands just as tall as the globe on top of the Von KleinSmid Center. More recently, the Dana & David Dornsife Cognitive Neuroscience Imaging Center was constructed in the base of the building.

In more recent years, construction of science buildings on USC's campus has slowed significantly. In 1987, the Hedco Fund donated money for the construction of the Hedco Neurosciences Building. Ground was broken on October 7, 1987, and the building was completed in early 1989. Like the Seeley G. Mudd Building, the Hedco Neurosciences Building was designed by the architectural firm of Grillias, Pirc, Rosier & Alves and cost $17.2 million to construct. That same year, Kaprielian Hall was constructed on the western edge of campus for use by the Engineering and Math Departments.

The following year, construction began on another building designed by the same architectural firm. The Hughes Aircraft Electrical Engineering Center, a six-story building equipped with state-of-the-art facilities, was the result of a $5 million donation from the Howard Hughes Corporation. The building was dedicated on September 14, 1991.

The most recent building to open as part of the Viterbi School of Engineering is Ronald Tutor Hall, which was begun in late 2003 and opened on February 2, 2005. The $50 million, six-story structure was partially funded by a $10 million grant from the building's namesake. Designed by A.C. Martin & Associates, Tutor Hall also features a café and lounge for students. Another recently constructed building is Ray R. Irani Hall, a molecular and computational biology center dedicated on February 9, 2007.

Student Housing

One of the first issues that President Topping had to deal with was student housing. In the northeast part of campus, von KleinSmid and Harris Residence Halls for women had been constructed in 1951; however, the need for even more housing was quickly becoming apparent. Ground was broken on October 28, 1957, for a new U-shaped addition to these dormitories, accommodating 228 additional women. The three-story buildings were designed by A.C. Martin & Associates as part of a $2.3 million investment in housing by the university (this cost would also cover a new men's dormitory).

Although initially scheduled to open in February 1959, construction was rushed in order for the halls to be open for the 1958 fall semester.

The building was expanded farther eastward in 1963, when David X. Marks donated $500,000 to construct two new wings, which were briefly known as Sarah Marks Hall. Today, Harris and University Residence Halls (to the north) are collectively known as North Residential College, while von KleinSmid and College Residence Halls (to the south) are known as New Residential College. These buildings are still used for undergraduate housing, although they are no longer exclusively for women.

Further expansion of this area of campus came in 1963, when a $500,000 gift from Mr. and Mrs. Michael C. Birnkrant was put toward a $1.75 million high-rise dormitory. Known as the Cecele and Michael C. Birnkrant Women's Residence Hall, the eight-story tower was designed by A.C. Martin & Associates and provided housing for 308 women. The building, which was dedicated on September 15, 1963, is still used for undergraduate housing.

While the women's residence halls were being expanded to the north, David X. Marks Residence Hall for men, built in 1953, was being added to as well. Originally constructed to house 50 students, it was announced in June 1957 that Marks had donated an additional $250,000 to double the capacity of the residence hall. This new addition was designed by James H. Van Dyke. Meanwhile, on the same day that ground was broken for the new women's housing in 1957, construction began on a new three-story, L-shaped building just east of Marks Hall, fronting Thirty-sixth and Figueroa Streets. Now known as Trojan Hall, the new building, designed by J.E. Stanton and William F. Stockwell, included rooms for 228 men. Both new men's residence halls were completed by August 1958, in time for the 1958 school year. Five years later, Stanton and Stockwell also designed an adjacent eight-story residence hall for 200 men. Known as David X. Marks Tower, this structure was open to students by October 1963.

In 1964, USC constructed a large complex of married student housing in the southwestern corner of campus. Consisting of seven buildings (three large apartment buildings and four smaller, freestanding housing units), the complex featured a Midcentury Modern design very typical of the period. More recently, all but two of the apartment buildings have been demolished and replaced by the International Residence College (2001) and the Parkside Residential Building (2006). The two 1964 apartment buildings are still also used as student housing.

Two of the tallest buildings on campus were constructed as student housing in 1972. Located along Jefferson Boulevard, Webb Tower and Fluor

Circa 1964 aerial view of USC's campus, looking northeast. The newly constructed Parkside Apartments can be seen in the foreground. Other recent developments that can be seen are Olin Hall of Engineering, the Ahmanson Center for Biological Research and Birnkrant Residence Hall. The Von KleinSmid Center is in its earliest stages of construction.

Tower (formerly known as Residence West) feature fourteen and eleven stories of housing, respectively. Fluor Tower was designed by Samuel E. Lunden and Joseph L. Johnson, who designed numerous other buildings on campus, while Webb Tower was designed by Dorman/Munselle Associates and constructed at a cost of $3.5 million. Between the two buildings, the Frank L. King Olympic Hall of Champions was erected in 1984, featuring dining and study space for students.

VON KLEINSMID CENTER COMPLEX

The most monumental building at USC during this time period is unquestionably the Von KleinSmid Center for International and Public

Affairs. USC's fifth president, Rufus B. von KleinSmid, was instrumental in creating the Schools of International Relations and Public Administration in 1924 and 1929, respectively, so it was a natural decision to name such a building in his honor. The site of the center, on the northeast corner of Thirty-fifth Place and University Avenue, was dedicated on June 27, 1964, to coincide with von KleinSmid's eighty-ninth birthday. The Trojan marching band played "Happy Birthday," and a cake was cut for the five hundred invited guests. Von KleinSmid, who was unable to attend due to a critical illness, listened to the ceremony on a special broadcast of KUSC radio station. An information building and Bacon Court (apartments for married students) were demolished to make way for the new center.

Noted American architect Edward Durell Stone was chosen to design the Von KleinSmid Center. One of the first major proponents of modernism in the United States, he designed the $3.1 million, three-story complex in the International style of architecture. The Von KleinSmid Center actually consists of three buildings under a single roof, giving them a sense of continuity. To the south, facing Alumni Park, is a three-story double arcade, with a large sunken courtyard in the center of the complex. Around the colonnade, flags are displayed of countries from which USC has students attending.

The most noticeable feature of the Von KleinSmid Center, however, is the 167-foot tower, topped with a 5,500-pound globe. While legend has it that von KleinSmid wanted the globe added to ensure that his namesake would remain the tallest building on campus, the truth is that the globe was inspired by a similar model at the 1964 New York World's Fair. In addition to housing the School of International Relations, the Department of Political Science and the School of Public Administration, the Von KleinSmid Center is also home to the Von KleinSmid Center Library for International and Public Affairs in its basement. By the time the center was dedicated on October 2, 1966, von KleinSmid had passed away more than two years earlier; however, the center is a spectacular tribute to a man who dedicated his entire life to the university.

The Von KleinSmid Center, however, was only the first step in the development of a larger complex in fulfillment of the university's 1961 master plan. Just to the north of the Von KleinSmid Center, work was soon begun on two additional buildings: Waite Phillips Hall of Education and the Social Sciences Building. Both of these were designed by Edward Durell Stone in the same style as the Von KleinSmid Center. The smaller of the two is the two-story Social Sciences Building, which was completed in early 1968 and houses the university's History Department.

The Von KleinSmid Center for International and Public Affairs, dedicated in October 1966. Designed by Edward Durell Stone, the building features a 167-foot tower, topped with a 5,500-pound globe. Behind the Von KleinSmid Center is Waite Phillips Hall, a twelve-story building that houses the Rossier School of Education. Between these two buildings is the Social Sciences Building.

The other, Waite Phillips Hall, has twelve stories and stands 156 feet tall. Architecturally identical to the Social Sciences Building, it houses the Rossier School of Education. Financed by a $3.5 million donation from the estate of the late oil magnate, the building opened to the public on May 12, 1968. Stone's two later buildings—the Social Sciences Building and Waite Phillips Hall—are connected by a sunken atrium, helping to unify the entire complex.

OTHER RECENT DEVELOPMENTS

Next door to USC's 1931 United University Church, a larger University Religious Center was constructed in 1965. Costing $425,000 (40 percent of which was covered by USC itself), the complex opened in October 1965 but was not dedicated until February of the following year.

In 1973, it was decided that the architecture and fine arts programs were in need of a new building. Work was soon begun on the Ray & Nadine Watt Hall of Architecture and Fine Arts. Located near Harris Hall, the Modernist building was designed primarily by Sam T. Hurst, with additional work by Killingsworth, Brary & Associates. Initial response to the $2.7 million structure, which was dedicated on May 14, 1974, was mixed. The *Los Angeles Times* referred to it as a "three-dimensional textbook on architecture"; however, it also pointed out many "pitfalls that should have been avoided."

Watt Hall includes the Helen Topping Architecture and Fine Arts Library, named after the late wife of USC president Norman Topping. The library underwent significant expansion in 1990, when the current sunlit atrium was added. Also in Watt Hall is Helen Lindhurst Fine Arts Gallery, established in 1979 to display the work of undergraduate students. Another building, the MacDonald Becket Center, was dedicated to the south of Watt Hall on March 20, 1993.

USC became one of the first institutions in America to have a center for gerontology research in 1964, when it founded the Ethel Percy Andrus Gerontology Center. Best known as the founder of the AARP, Andrus was a USC graduate herself. In early 1972, it was announced that a $3.5 million building would be constructed for the center. Designed by Edward Durell Stone, who also designed the Von KleinSmid Center complex, the three-story building surrounds a large central courtyard. It was dedicated on February 12, 1973. Two years later, USC would found the Leonard Davis School of Gerontology, which was the first program in the world to offer a PhD in gerontology.

In the late 1960s, USC began to expand its business school's facilities. Ground was broken on May 26, 1965, on H. Leslie Hoffman Hall of Business Administration, located along Exposition Boulevard behind Bridge Hall (to which it is connected by a series of walkways). The eight-story, $3.4 million tower was designed by famed Chinese American architect I.M. Pei. The building was dedicated on May 16, 1967, after nearly two years of construction. The large auditorium in the building was funded by Southern California Edison, the eighty-five-thousand-volume library was supplied by banker Roy P. Crocker and an executive conference suite was donated by the Times Mirror Company.

In addition to expanding the business school, USC also expanded the scope of its law school. Nearby, Hoffman Hall, the site of the Elvon and Mabel Musick Law Building was dedicated on April 20, 1969; the finished building was opened on February 12, 1971. Designed by A.C. Martin & Associates, the

The Ethel Percy Andrus Gerontology Center, constructed in 1973 to house one of the nation's first gerontology programs. This three-story building was designed by Edward Durell Stone, who was also responsible for the Von KleinSmid Center.

H. Leslie Hoffman Hall of Business Administration, constructed between 1965 and 1967, was designed by I.M. Pei, one of the most famous architects of the twentieth century. The eight-story building is unique in that it is one of the few on USC's campus that doesn't feature exterior brickwork.

$3.4 million building also houses the Asa V. Call Law Library. In 1985, a four-thousand-square-foot addition was added to the east side of the Musick Law Building, greatly increasing the capabilities of USC's law program.

The USC Sol Price School of Public Policy (formerly known as the School of Policy, Planning and Development) broke ground for the Ralph and Goldy Lewis Hall on May 24, 1995. The building, which was dedicated on August 27, 1999, was designed by the architectural firm of Zimmer, Gunsul and Frasca. Nearby, Popovich Hall opened as part of the Marshall School of Business in the fall of 1999. Named after alumni Jane Hoffman Popovich and J. Kristoffer Popovich, who donated $5 million of the building's $19.8 million cost, the building added fifty-five thousand square feet to the business school.

Although established in 1936, USC's School of Library Science didn't have its own building until October 3, 1974, when the Montgomery Ross Fisher Building was dedicated. The $1 million, three-story building was designed by Robert E. Donald & Associates. More recently, the building has become part of the School of Social Work; an additional, adjacent Social Work Center was constructed in 2003.

USC was the home of the first conference center on the West Coast to be built in an urban setting. On September 30, 1976, the $2.5 million Davidson Conference Center for Continuing Education opened. Like many buildings from the era, it was designed by Edward Durell Stone. The center, which can accommodate 650 people, is unique in that it wasn't constructed in a remote area but instead in the center of a major city. The highlight of the building is a seventy-five-foot tower with the USC seal on it.

USC's Annenberg School for Communication and Journalism was founded in 1971 with the support of philanthropist and ambassador Walter Annenberg. One of USC's most well-respected schools, the school describes its faculty and students as "defining communication and journalism for the 21st century and beyond." The building in which the school currently resides was opened in November 1976, due in large part to a $4.5 million grant from Annenberg. Located in Founders Park, the building was designed by A. Quincy Jones & Associates.

Beginning in 1965, USC began to expand the facilities of its music program. The first building constructed for this purpose was the Mrs. Willis H. Booth Ferris Rehearsal Hall, located near Taper Hall. Nine years later, in 1974, the Virginia Ramo Hall of Music was added to the complex, to be followed the next year by the Albert S. Raubenheimer Music Faculty Memorial Building. In 1976, the last building to be added, the Bing Theater, was constructed. All of these buildings were designed by William L. Pereira,

USC's Annenberg School for Communication and Journalism, constructed in 1976. The building is located in Founders Park, not far from where USC's first building sat in 1880. Designed by A. Quincy Jones & Associates, the building is typical of those constructed on USC's campus during the 1970s.

also responsible for many other buildings on campus. One building from this era that no longer exists, the Arnold Schoenberg Institute, was constructed in 1973 to house the famed Austrian composer's archives. The structure was demolished to make way for the new Cinematic Arts complex.

In 1980, as part of USC's 100th-anniversary celebration, Grace Ford Salvatori Hall of Journalism, Speech and Linguistics was officially opened. Dedicated in November 1980, the building still houses offices and classrooms from USC's Dornsife College of Letters, Arts and Sciences.

Two large buildings were completed in 1989. The first of these is the General William Lyon University Center, which features USC's gymnasium and intramural recreation facilities. The other, located in the heart of campus, is the Pertusati University Bookstore, designed by the architectural firm of Grillias, Pirc, Rosier & Alves.

Construction continues as rapidly as ever on USC's campus. In May 2008, ground was broken for the new Ronald Tutor Campus Center, which replaced the USC Commons and Norman Topping Student Activities Center. The building was dedicated on August 26, 2010, by President Nikias. More recently, construction was started in the fall of 2012 on Wallis Annenberg Hall and Verna and Peter Dauterive Hall, both of which are expected to be completed in the fall of 2014.

Chapter 4

EXPOSITION PARK

THE FOUNDING OF EXPOSITION PARK

Exposition Park is a 160-acre plot of land directly to the south of the University of Southern California; it is bordered by Martin Luther King Jr. Boulevard to the south, Figueroa Street to the east, Vermont Avenue to the west and Exposition Boulevard to the north. Dating back to 1872, it is one of the oldest parks in Los Angeles and continues to be a popular destination to this day.

The land was originally purchased for $6,000 by the Southern District Agricultural Society in 1872 and called Agricultural Park, a name that would stick for almost four decades. Between 1872 and 1879, the land was the home of an agricultural fairground for the newly developing surrounding neighborhoods, promoting a shift from the former "rancho" system that characterized California to a more structured farming system. The project soon went bankrupt, however, and the land was taken over by opportunists who realized that the park sat just outside Los Angeles's official city limits. Quickly, the land was filled with brothels, saloons, gambling halls and a large racetrack (complete with a four-story brick grandstand that contained "the city's longest bar") that hosted everything from horses to greyhounds, dromedary camels, bicycles and cars.

Without any jurisdiction from the city itself, gambling and prostitution flourished in Agricultural Park, gaining the park a reputation as a Wild West town of sorts. A large wooden fence was even constructed around the park, shutting off the seedy businesses from the outside world. The original grandstand

An extremely early photo (circa 1880s) of Agricultural Park's racetrack before the park had been redeveloped into Exposition Park. The racetrack, which was demolished in 1909, featured everything from horse to bicycle to camel races, in addition to containing "the city's longest bar." *Photo courtesy of the University of Southern California archives.*

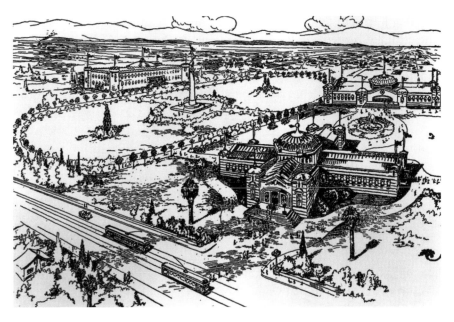

A rare 1909 concept drawing of Exposition Park. While vastly different from what was actually constructed a few years later, a similar layout of the three buildings was adopted. The architecture in this drawing is reminiscent of other expositions from the early twentieth century; however, the large-scale exposition that many citizens hoped for never ended up materializing. *Photo courtesy of the Los Angeles Times archive.*

and hotel stood approximately where the Natural History Museum is today, on the northwestern side of the racetrack. The park was so popular that the Main St. & Agricultural Park Railroad opened in 1875 and continued to service the park from downtown until the 1890s, operating nineteen trains at its peak.

Around the time that Agricultural Park began to slide into disarray, USC opened just blocks to the north, bringing in many prominent (and oftentimes religious) Los Angeles citizens to the neighborhood. Social outcry was spearheaded by USC law professor William M. Bowen (who was almost singlehandedly responsible for the development of Exposition Park a decade later), in 1898, when he realized his students were skipping Sunday school to gamble and loiter at the park. Bowen's actions forced the City of Los Angeles to annex Agricultural Park on June 12, 1899; this same annexation is what made USC part of Los Angeles proper. Now the city was empowered to crack down on the gambling, prostitution and all-around mayhem that existed in the park.

Despite Bowen's work, the 1900s decade saw a continuation of craziness in the park. In 1903, ten thousand people gathered to watch Barney Oldfield break the land speed record—a mile in fifty-five seconds—and in 1906, a mile of train track was laid for a demolition derby of two steam engines traveling head-on at fifty miles per hour. By 1908, after a long dispute over who actually owned the land (apparently, the State of California owned it all along but still ended up purchasing it from the latest tenant), Bowen (alongside USC president George F. Bovard and other local elites) began to lay out the plans that would shape the park into what it is today. The first phase, located in the northern part of the old Agricultural Park, was to consist of three buildings—a museum, exposition building and state armory—surrounding a sunken garden.

In January 1909, the State of California allotted $600,000 to the area, which would be renamed Exposition Park on December 17, 1910, and the City of Los Angeles became transfixed with developing it. Within days, there were conceptual drawings, architectural ideas and even plans for a massive, four-month exposition in 1913 (which never ended up materializing). The Exposition Building was set to be the centerpiece of the park, and $250,000 was set aside upfront for its construction. Approximately $150,000 was allocated for a museum that would showcase the natural history of Southern California, as well as fine arts and the cultural history of Los Angeles; $100,000 was provided for the State Armory Building (which would be the first armory in the state); and an additional $100,000 ($10,000 per year for ten years) was granted for general landscaping of the park. The Exposition Building and Museum were to be run by the county, the Armory by the state and the park itself by the City of Los Angeles, The original Agricultural Park buildings were torn down between April and May 1909, and construction on both the Exposition Building and the Historical and Art Museum began soon after.

THE STATE EXPOSITION BUILDING

The Exposition Building was set to be the crown jewel of W.M. Bowen's Exposition Park. He envisioned a European-style exposition in which all fifty-eight of California's counties would provide exhibits detailing their agriculture and industry. As a whole, these exhibits would highlight California's unique place in the country. Construction of the building began in July 1910, the same time as the museum, located diagonally across the Rose Garden.

The building, also known as Bowen Hall, consisted of a large central hall with wings at either end, forming a large U shape with an open courtyard to the south. By May 3, 1911, the building was more or less complete but did not have electricity or any of the proposed exhibits. It would take until February 27, 1912, for W.M. Bowen himself to turn the electric lights on for the first time and invite neighborhood residents inside for a tour. Display pieces and cases were just starting to arrive, and over the next few months the exposition filled up, with each county providing its own display.

As time went on, many people felt that the California State Exposition was outdated, as exhibits included things as mundane as ears of corn and jars of jam. The building was remodeled in 1949, and in 1951 it reopened as the California Museum of Science and Industry. New exhibits included a revamped Agricultural Hall, an Industry Hall, a Transportation Hall featuring the world's largest model train display, a Marine Room with models of California's harbors, a Water Resources Exhibit, a Mineral Hall and a Forest, Parks and Recreation Exhibit (including a separate "Redwood Empire Room").

Over the years, these exhibits expanded and changed; some of the more memorable were the large egg-shaped chick incubator, the General Motors–sponsored "Turing Wheel" exhibit on the history of automobiles and the diorama of Ben Franklin flying his kite in the Electricity Hall. On May 29, 1957, a large Horticultural Hall was built between the two original wings of the museum, filling in what had been the large courtyard. This new building, which featured an extremely large window as its south wall to allow in natural light, would be the host of numerous botanical displays and festivities over the years, before being renamed Edgerton Hall and converted

into more exhibition space. Eventually, a large, enclosed courtyard was built to the south of the Horticultural Hall.

The museum continued to expand four years later, when on March 23, 1961, a new science wing opened to the east of the original building. This made the Museum of Science and Architecture the second-largest museum of its kind in the world. This building, with its unique barrel-vaulted roof (the largest of its kind when built), is now an administrative building but for decades held many hands-on science-themed exhibits, including the fondly remembered "Mathematica" (which used interactive displays to teach people advanced mathematical concepts).

Further expansion eastward came on June 27, 1968, when the Hall of Health opened after four years of planning. Heralded as the first building in the world constructed specifically for a museum about the human body, exhibits included "Clearissa the Transparent Woman," a woman lacking skin and muscle so that people could see how the internals of the human body worked. In conjunction with the Hall of Health, the Kinsey Auditorium, a five-hundred-seat theater, was also built as part of the museum. Today, both of these buildings still stand to the east of the California Science Center.

The 1984 Olympics provided a huge growth opportunity for all of Exposition Park, and the Museum of Science and Industry was no exception. Initial plans in the early 1980s included a multicultural center to the west of the museum (which ultimately was never built), as well as a new Aerospace Building, IMAX theater and Air and Space Garden (more on these buildings later). A new addition to the museum itself was the Mark Taper Hall of Economics and Finance, which opened in April 1985 to the south of the original Exposition Building. This was billed as the first museum in the world focused solely on economics, and much like the other exhibits, it presented advanced concepts in a way that was accessible to children and adults alike.

Opposite, top: An early exterior view of the California State Exposition Building, also known as Bowen Hall. Opened for the first time on February 27, 1912, the Exposition Building was initially imagined as a showcase for all of California's fifty-eight counties. Today, only the historic façade of the building remains intact. *Photo courtesy of the Los Angeles Public Library.*

Opposite, bottom: A plaque on the outside of the State Exposition Building, stating its initial intent. In 1951, the building became the California Museum of Science and Industry, and it more recently reopened as the California Science Center in 1998. However, many of the center's current exhibits harken back to exhibits from the building's earliest days. *Photo courtesy of the Los Angeles Public Library.*

The California Museum of Science and Industry closed its doors in 1996. The original Exposition Building, Bowen Hall, was almost entirely torn down—today, all that remains is the historic façade. The new Howard F. Ahmanson Building opened in February 1998 as the California Science Center. The exhibits in the new center are similar in many ways to those at the Museum of Science and Industry; "World of Life" and "Creative World" are reminiscent of the old Hall of Health and Turning Wheel exhibitions. Further expansion of the California Science Center came in 2010, with the opening of the "Ecosystems" exhibit, and in 2012, when the center received space shuttle *Endeavour* from NASA.

The Museum of Natural History

Ground was broken for the Museum of History, Science and Art on July 11, 1910. In March of that year, a board of directors had been chosen for the museum, comprising representatives of the Historical Society of Southern California, the Southern California Academy of Sciences, the Cooper Ornithological Club and the Fine Arts League. These disparate organizations all needed a public place to display their collections and came together to fill the museum building once it was constructed. Frank S. Daggett, a well-known naturalist in the area, was appointed the first director of the museum.

The cornerstone was laid on December 10, 1910, and a little more than a year later (December 26, 1911), a nest and eggs from a goldfinch became the first recorded gift to the museum. The building itself was completed in early 1912, at a final cost of $226,000. The board of directors toured the building for the first time on July 31, 1912, when exhibits were first starting to be installed.

Although quietly opened to the public by early July 1913, the ceremonial grand opening of the museum took place on November 6, 1913. This event, which attracted thirty-five thousand people, also featured the breaking of a bottle of Owens River water to celebrate the opening of the Los Angeles Aqueduct and the laying of the cornerstone for the State Armory.

The building initially consisted of a large central rotunda, seventy-five feet wide and fifty-eight feet tall, surrounded by three wings for exhibits. The rotunda, which also served as the entrance between 1913 and 1930, is to this day the focal point of the museum, featuring marble walls twenty feet high, a twenty-foot stained-glass skylight and the larger-than-life statue *Three Muses* by Julia Bracken Wendt (which was the first piece of public art funded by Los

A photo of the cornerstone-laying ceremony for the Natural History Museum on November 10, 1910. The museum would open slightly less than three years later, on November 6, 1913. Initially consisting of only three wings surrounding a central rotunda, the museum has been expanded substantially over the years. *Photo courtesy of the University of Southern California archives.*

A view of the Museum of History, Science and Art shortly after its completion in 1913. The famed Rose Garden in front of the museum wouldn't be planted for another fourteen years. Today, the building serves as the Natural History Museum of Los Angeles County, still maintaining its original purpose a century after it was begun. *Photo courtesy of the University of Southern California archives.*

Angeles County). Around the large dome, four smaller domes were built to contain offices and collections rooms. The three large wings of the building each held a different department's exhibits: history to the north, science to the south and art in the western wing.

The north and south wings—history and science, respectively—feature identical architecture. These wings were built with suspended balconies that serve as additional exhibition space, and large skylights provide the halls with natural light. The history wing, run by the Southern California Historical Society, featured many relics of California's early days, as well as having an extensive library on the history of the state located upstairs. The science wing housed the large bird, insect and other zoological collections that were donated to the museum early on, in addition to the spectacular ice age fossils that were being excavated ten miles away at the La Brea Tar Pits.

The art wing of the museum, perpendicular to the other two, was the last gallery to be filled. This wing differs from the other two in that it was only one floor and did not have a glass ceiling. When the museum opened in 1913, there were 170 pieces of art on display, including a Raphael self-portrait.

The museum was such a success that by 1925, a new wing was built between the science and art wings, effectively quadrupling the museum's original thirty thousand square feet. This new floor space allowed the museum to expand its exhibits to include things such as the North American Mammal Halls, which are still in their original locations today. On November 7, 1930, the day after the seventeenth anniversary of the museum, another addition opened, this time nearly doubling the size of the museum. It was at this time that the front entrance to the museum was moved from the rotunda to the south lawn, where it is today.

This new addition included the large central hall that today features a fighting tyrannosaurus and triceratops, as well as the African Mammal Hall and other exhibit spaces. By this point, all of the departments of the museum were expanding greatly, with the Zoology Department leading expeditions around the world to collect specimens, the Paleontology Department continuing to excavate fossils from the tar pits and the History and Art Departments frequently changing their exhibits, including antique car displays and a Claude Monet exhibition. Further expansion of the museum occurred in 1960, when an auditorium was added to the west end, and 1976, by which time all of the current exhibit halls were completed.

Today, the museum appears much as it would have in its early years. The rotunda has undergone multiple renovations to restore it to its 1913 appearance, and the three original halls all feature newly redesigned exhibits—prehistoric mammals in the old history hall, the history of Los Angeles in the art hall and dinosaurs in the science hall (which also extends into the 1925 portion of the building).

THE EXPOSITION PARK ROSE GARDEN

Despite the construction of the Museum and Exposition Building, it took more than two years of deliberation to come up with plans for the land in between them. Finally, on March 29, 1911, final plans for the landscaping of the park were decided on. Because the opening of Exposition Park was set to coincide with the opening of the Los Angeles Aqueduct, nearly all early plans called for a monument to be erected in the center of the park to commemorate this event. Wilbur David Cook Jr. proposed that a sunken garden be constructed between the newly finished Historical and Art Museum and the as-yet-to-be-built State Armory. Early plans called for everything from a large lagoon to a one-hundred-foot fountain in the center of the sunken garden. However, all that was actually constructed in 1913 was a brick wall surrounding the area. In May 1914, it was announced that the garden would be filled with wildflowers, but these plans did not come to fruition until 1921, when yearly flower shows began to be held. There were also unsuccessful plans for a permanent horticultural building in the park.

The rose garden that exists today was begun on July 1, 1927, when fifteen thousand roses consisting of over one hundred varieties were planted in the sunken garden. The planting was completed by April 1928, and although none of the original bushes survives, many from the 1940s and '50s can still be seen. Approximately 166 concrete beds were constructed, as well as a central lily pond (later to be converted into the current fountain), four gazebos and concrete walkways. Topsoil was even brought in from Griffith Park. From its inception, it was heralded as the largest rose garden in the world and proved to be a popular tourist attraction. In 1932, relief-figures designed to celebrate the Olympic Games were added to the north end of the garden, along with Art Deco streetlamps that are still standing.

Despite its initial popularity, once the Great Depression struck the country, the garden was looked at as trivial by some, and in late 1933, the City of Los Angeles had to ask the county for $7,500 to keep it open. Another threat faced the Rose Garden in 1986, when a football practice field or an underground parking garage were proposed on the site. Local outcry and media coverage stopped the plans quickly, though, and by 1991 the Rose Garden was listed on the National Register of Historic Places, safe from any future development in the area.

THE STATE ARMORY

Plans for a State Armory building in Exposition Park had been circulating from the earliest days of the park's development in 1909, and funds were allocated for such a building from the start. Due to architectural and political issues, though, the actual construction took much longer than expected. The first design that was proposed differed drastically from the finished product

Exposition Park's State Armory. Constructed between 1912 and 1914, it was the last of Exposition Park's three buildings to be completed. Through World War II, the building housed the 7th Infantry Regiment (later the 160th Infantry Regiment). Today, the Armory building serves as an annex for the California Science Center. *Photo courtesy of the Los Angeles Public Library.*

(featuring a large tower with battlements), but the final plans were debuted in August 1912 by architect J.W. Wollett.

Described at the time as the "finest armory in the country," his building would be 280 feet by 212 feet, have a concrete and steel frame and be covered in red brick with a stone entryway. Initially, it consisted of two separate buildings (a front administrative building and living quarters in the rear), separated by a large drill floor for military exercises (in the late 1920s, this central portion was enclosed but retained a similar purpose). The Armory would also be home to a field hospital, a war college, an arsenal, shooting ranges and a public recreation hall.

Construction began on November 23, 1912, at a cost of $250,000. Although there was a cornerstone-laying ceremony put on by the Freemasons on November 7, 1913, the building was not functional until July 29, 1914, when a crowd of 1,500 civilians and 400 soldiers gathered to celebrate the official opening. From the time of its construction through World War II, the building was home to the 7th Infantry Regiment (later to become the 160th Infantry Regiment), and troops would frequently march through the city streets or train in surrounding areas early on.

Beginning in the 1920s, the building was host to a large number of nonmilitary events as well, including a food exposition in 1924, wresting matches in 1925, a poultry show and a rabbit show in 1929, fencing in the 1932 Olympic Games, annual hot rod shows in the 1940s and '50s, a model plane meet in 1950 and the First Annual World Plastics Fair and Expo in 1955, in addition to local science fairs and political rallies. Perhaps the largest civilian operation to take place in the Armory was the 1947 American Bowling Congress tournament, in which thirty-six lanes were constructed and four thousand teams participated, including a special appearance by silent film star Harold Lloyd.

As part of the renovation of Exposition Park in anticipation for the 1984 Olympic Games, a relatively unknown architect named Frank Gehry was commissioned to design a new Aerospace Building for the Museum of Science and Industry on the south side of the Armory Building. This was Gehry's first large public work; he would go on to become one of the most famous contemporary architects in the world, designing such buildings as the Walt Disney Concert Hall in downtown Los Angeles. Construction started in 1982, complete with a Lockheed F104 Starfighter jet precipitously balanced on the building's façade. Up until July 2011, the building was filled with airplanes, satellites and other displays detailing the history of aerospace travel from the Wright Brothers through the present day. These exhibits have since been moved into the Ahmanson Building at the Science Center. One of the more interesting exhibits in the old Aerospace Building was "Windows on the Universe," an audio-visual experience detailing the birth of the universe and the history of space travel with a script written by Ray Bradbury.

Shortly after the Aerospace Building opened, the Armory building itself was converted into the Space Building, in which more aircraft were displayed. Completing the space-themed section of the Museum of Science and Industry were the Mitsubishi IMAX Theater (a new IMAX theater is now a part of the California Science Center) and the Corwin D. Denney Air and Space Garden, in which DC-3 and DC-8 aircraft were displayed on the back patio of the Armory. Although this area has since been converted into the Theodore Alexander Jr. Science Center School, the DC-8 jet can still be seen off Figueroa Boulevard.

Today, the former State Armory building is operated by the California Science Center as the Wallis Annenberg Building for Science Learning and Innovation. The former drill floor has become the open-air "Big Lab" for use by students and teachers at local schools, and the two halves of the building contain classrooms and laboratories.

OTHER EXPOSITION PARK ATTRACTIONS

The most recent addition to the lineup of Exposition Park's museums is the California African American Museum. Initially founded in 1981, it was housed in the California Museum of Science and Industry until July 1984, when the current museum building opened. Located between the Armory and Exposition Buildings, it features three galleries of rotating exhibits documenting the role of African Americans in culture, from politics to sports to entertainment. The building underwent a massive renovation between 2001 and 2003, and future plans include expanding the current building to three stories

Arguably the most famous building in Exposition Park is the Los Angeles Memorial Coliseum, constructed between 1921 and 1923. The only stadium in the world to host two Olympic Games (1932 and 1984), it has also held countless other events over the years. The Coliseum, along with the 1932 Olympic Swimming Stadium and the Los Angeles Memorial Sports Arena, are discussed in-depth in the "Sports at University Park" chapter.

In front of the Los Angeles Coliseum sits a palm tree that some claim is the oldest tree in Los Angeles. Probably born in the 1850s, it was moved to San Pedro Street (now in Little Tokyo) in the latter part of that decade. On July 26, 1888, the palm was transported to the entrance of the Southern Pacific Railroad's Arcade Station downtown, where it sat until the station's demolition in 1914. At that point, preservationists succeeded in moving the tree to Exposition Park, where it has thrived ever since.

In addition to the aforementioned buildings, Exposition Park has been home to many other attractions. After construction started in the north of the park in 1910, the old racetrack was moved to the south of the Exposition Building. Although W.M. Bowen was opposed to the racetrack from the start, it had to be kept, at least for a short time, in order to appease lawmakers who were worried about losing revenue. Instead of cutting diagonally through the park as it had previously, it was laid out so that the long stretches of the track ran east and west, parallel to Martin Luther King Jr. Boulevard. A large, concrete grandstand was placed at the southern edge of the track, alongside stables and maintenance buildings. Interestingly, when construction started on the Los Angeles Memorial Coliseum a decade later, the stadium was placed inside the still-extant racetrack, which was removed shortly thereafter.

Exposition Park also featured a large bandstand directly to the west of the Exposition Building, which was used for, among other things, concerts, speakers and an annual Easter Sunrise Service. On the opposite side of

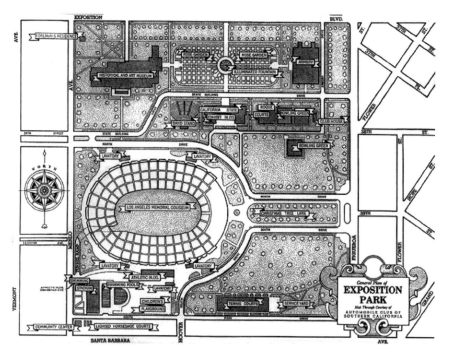

A 1932 map of Exposition Park, showing the Rose Garden, Natural History Museum, Armory and Exposition Building to the north. The Coliseum, in addition to a number of other sporting facilities, can also be seen. Today, much of the park remains unchanged from how it appeared in its earliest days.

the Exposition Building were croquet fields, horseshoe pits and an athletic clubhouse (which stood until the African American Museum was built in the 1980s). Another 1920s clubhouse, listed as a Los Angeles Historic-Cultural Monument, still stands in the southwest corner of the park.

Chapter 5

NORTH UNIVERSITY PARK

HISTORIC HOMES

The North University Park neighborhood shares much of its history with the University of Southern California. Just north of USC's campus, North University Park had been agricultural land before development began in the late nineteenth century. Today, North University Park features one of the richest collections of historic architecture in the entire city, including numerous Victorian and Craftsman-style homes dating back to the 1800s.

Land was subdivided into housing plots beginning in 1885, shortly after the founding of the university. The West Adams district had already been established as the wealthiest neighborhood in Los Angeles (the "Beverly Hills of its day"), so the construction of a neighborhood between West Adams and the newly founded USC seemed natural. Early on, many wealthy Los Angeles businessmen and politicians, as well as professors from USC, moved into the region. By 1888, homes were selling for $3,000. Streetcars linked the suburb to downtown in 1891, further prompting growth until the entire region was developed in 1901.

Today, although the neighborhood is roughly bounded by Jefferson Boulevard to the south, Vermont Avenue to the west, Adams Boulevard to the north and Figueroa Street to the east, a vast majority of the historic homes are situated between Vermont and Hoover. This area has recently been divided into two districts recognized by the National Register of Historic Places: the Menlo Avenue–West Twenty-ninth Street Historic

District (located to the west, toward Vermont) and the North University Park Historic District (located to the east, toward Hoover). While the number of architecturally significant homes is too large to cover in any detail, there are a number of houses that have unique cultural and historical importance.

One of the oldest houses in North University Park is the Miller and Herriott House (1163 West Twenty-seventh Street), constructed in 1890. A combination of the Stick and Eastlake Victorian styles of architecture, this house is particularly interesting because, when the land was originally being settled, developers used it as the model home to attract buyers to the neighborhood. Today, the home is used as housing for USC students.

The William W. Cockins House (2653 South Hoover Street) is a late Queen Anne–style home that is heralded by architects as one of the finest examples of the style in the city. Built in 1894, it was converted to a boardinghouse not long after its construction. Allegedly, Charlie Chaplin rented a room in this home when he moved to Los Angeles for the first time in 1913; there's even a mannequin of the Tramp on the second-story balcony. This house has been operated by USC since 1999 as the Center for Occupation and Lifestyle Redesign. Nearby is West Adams Gardens (1158–1176 West Adams Boulevard), one of the earliest gated communities in Los Angeles. Constructed in 1920, it is a collection of seven identical apartment buildings built in a striking Tudor revival style.

Although not as physically impressive as some of its neighbors, the building at 2639 Monmouth Avenue is one of the more historic homes in the area. On February 5, 1900, Adlai E. Stevenson II was born in this 1894 Queen Anne–style home. Stevenson is best remembered as the Democratic nominee for president in 1952 and 1956 (losing both times to Dwight D. Eisenhower); he also served as the governor of Illinois from 1949 to 1953 and the U.S. ambassador to the United Nations from 1961 to 1965. It was after his death in 1965 that this house was declared a Los Angeles Historic-Cultural Monument.

Almost certainly the oldest house in North University Park spent the first century of its existence about a mile north of its current location. The Forthmann House, currently the sixth-oldest home in Los Angeles, was built in 1887 on West Eighteenth Street near Figueroa. John A. Forthmann, a German soap manufacturer, commissioned Burgess J. Reeve to design the Victorian mansion, which is a mixture of many styles, including Eastlake and Italianate. In 1989, the house was relocated to its current location, 2801 South Hoover Boulevard, to prevent its destruction during the building of the new LA Convention Center. Along the way, streetlamps had to be removed as the house was too wide, and it was actually cheaper to replace the lamps than to modify the house. Today, it is owned and operated by USC as the Community House, having also been the home of real estate developers, campus security and the LA Police Department.

THE WEST ADAMS CORRIDOR

In addition to dozens of historic houses, North University Park is also home to many other cultural and historic landmarks. With the large influx of residents at the turn of the twentieth century, there was a need for schools, churches, performance venues and other civic infrastructure. Many of these buildings have stood the test of time and are now celebrated as some of Los Angeles's most historic landmarks.

One building that can be seen from miles away is the Second Church of Christ, Scientist, located at 946 West Adams Boulevard. Although the Second Church congregation was established in Los Angeles in 1898, it took until March 1908 for the cornerstone of the building to be laid). Designed by Alfred F. Rosenheim, it has been called the finest example of Neoclassical architecture in all of Los Angeles. The church opened its doors for service for the first time in January 1910. Modeled somewhat after the Christian Scientist Mother Church in Boston, it features a seventy-foot-wide copper-covered dome, mahogany woodwork and a white-glazed brick exterior; in fact, at the time of its completion, the *Los Angeles Times* claimed it was the most expensive church on the West Coast. Originally built to seat 1,200 people, it served as a Christian Science Church all the way up until 2007, at which point the congregation had become too small to warrant such an extravagant building. In 2009, it was purchased by the Art of Living Foundation and today serves as a community center and administrative center for the group.

Located in the shadow of the Second Church of Christ, Scientist, is the building with perhaps the most varied history in the area: Sunshine Mission (also affectionately known as Casa de Rosas due to the large number of roses formerly along its walls and courtyard). Located at 2608 South Hoover Street (at Adams Boulevard), Sunshine Mission is actually a collection of four buildings, the oldest and most prominent of which was built in 1893. It was the first building designed by Sumner P. Hunt, who would go on to design other Los Angeles landmarks such as the Automobile Club building,

The Second Church of Christ, Scientist, which opened in 1910, was the most expensive church on the West Coast when it was constructed. Its copper dome is seventy feet wide, and the entire building is covered in white-glazed brick. Today, the building is owned by the Art of Living Foundation. *Photo courtesy of the University of Southern California archives.*

located just a few blocks away. Sunshine Mission is important architecturally because it is one of the earliest examples of Mission revival architecture; it is also one of the finest surviving examples of the style in Southern California.

The main building was built as the home of the Froebel Institute. Friedrich Froebel, who lived from 1782 to 1852, was a German pedagogue who developed the concept of kindergarten. This makes Casa de Rosas one of the earliest kindergartens in California; it would take the state another six years to make it part of public school curriculum. The building nearly burned down in 1903, however, and was reopened in 1904 as the prestigious Girls Collegiate Boarding School. This school was responsible for building the other three buildings that make up the complex; they were originally constructed as dormitories, a gymnasium and classrooms.

By the 1930s, Casa de Rosas was functioning as a hotel and restaurant (featuring complete dinners for fifty cents and filet mignon for sixty-five cents); this is also where the international student population of USC lived at the time. It was again repurposed in the early 1940s, when it was used as barracks for soldiers in World War II. After being put up for sale, it was purchased in November 1950 by L. Ron Hubbard as a center for his Dianetic Research Foundation. Making the most of the building's many small rooms (formerly dormitories and hotel rooms), as well as the large auditorium, Hubbard often held demonstrations and classes (charging up to $500 for a twenty-five-hour session).

The building changed hands for the last time in late 1950, when Sister Essie Binkley West purchased it. West, known as the "Angel of Skid Row," had been helping needy young women and unwed mothers for decades. Despite decades of dilapidation and disrepair, as well as two arson attempts in 1984 and 1987, the building still serves as a shelter for women today, carrying on the legacy that Sister West established over half a century ago.

Spencer Tracy was ranked the ninth most iconic actor of all time by the American Film Institute and is perhaps best known for starring alongside Katharine Hepburn in movies such as *Adam's Rib* and *Guess Who's Coming to Dinner*. In 1924, Spencer and his wife, Louise Treadwell, gave birth to a son, John, who was declared nerve deaf. Louise began searching desperately for a cure for her son but was told that the only hope for John was if he could learn to lip read. This started Louise on a crusade for hearing-impaired children that would last the rest of her life. In 1942, the year after her husband began his long-term public affair with Katherine Hepburn, Louise spoke at USC about her experiences with John. After meeting with many parents of deaf children, she decided to establish the John Tracy Clinic later that year.

As an interesting aside, the clinic, located at 806 West Adams Boulevard, replaced the home of famed abolitionist and woman suffragette Caroline Severance, who had lived there from 1875 until her death in 1914. Her tiny house, known to visitors as the Red Roof (and later *El Nido*, meaning "The Nest"), was described in 1906 as "a rendezvous for literary people visiting Los Angeles." Severance became a sort of spiritual leader for any and all

L. Ron Hubbard, founder of Scientology, is seen conducting a Dianetics seminar in Casa de Rosas in November 1950. Casa de Rosas, constructed in 1893 by Sumner P. Hunt, is one of the most architecturally significant buildings in University Park. At various times, it has served as a school, restaurant, hotel and women's shelter.

progressive movements in Southern California. Having fought for suffrage for over six decades, she was finally able to cast her first vote (for Theodore Roosevelt) in 1912, at the age of ninety-two. The cross street of Adams, where the house was located, is still known as Severance Street, in honor of Caroline's social justice work.

The John Tracy Clinic, established in 1942 on USC's campus, was initially funded solely by Spencer Tracy, despite being estranged from his wife. Regardless of his regular affairs, he was always supportive of his wife, donating over half a million dollars to the clinic over the course of his life and bringing media attention to her cause. At the dedication of the current facility in 1952, he famously said, "There's nothing I've ever done that can match what Louise has done for deaf children and their parents." Another early board member and supporter was Walt Disney. Louise continued to expand the clinic until her death in 1983, receiving honorary degrees from multiple schools (including USC) and widespread acclaim. To this day, the John Tracy Clinic continues to offer free hearing screenings, family services and education to children with hearing impairments; each year, twenty-five thousand children worldwide are served by the clinic.

Farther east on West Adams Boulevard is the Automobile Club of Southern California headquarters (2601 South Figueroa Street), constructed between 1921 and 1923. Founded in 1900, Automobile Club of Southern California membership was already up to fifty-six thousand by the time the building opened. The headquarters housed all administrative facilities, in addition to providing members with locker rooms, dining rooms and a smoking lounge. Designed by Sumner P. Hunt and Silas R. Burns, it is a large, rectangular-shaped Spanish Colonial revival building around a central courtyard that is now used for parking. Today, although still the Automobile Club Los Angeles Branch Office, the building is open to the public, featuring a beautiful three-story rotunda, a large-scale relief map of California from 1920, original El Camino Real mission bells and a cross section of a 1,450-year-old giant sequoia.

The Automobile Club of Southern California played a huge role in the early development of Los Angeles. Early functions of the club included having a safety patrol (before the California Highway Patrol was established), setting speed limits within the city (originally eight miles per hour in residential districts, six miles per hour in business districts and four miles per hour in intersections) and placing road signs along highways. Perhaps one of the greatest achievements of the club was placing the first traffic light in Los Angeles in 1924 at the intersection of Figueroa and Adams, the busiest intersection in the nation at that time. Traffic signals had previously been installed downtown but did not feature the prominent red and green lights that have become so familiar today. This first installation resembled a train signal more than anything else but was replaced by a more modern traffic light in 1930.

Across the street from the Automobile Club building is St. John's Cathedral, an Episcopalian church located at 514 West Adams Boulevard. The original St. John's Cathedral was a striking neo-Gothic building built on the same site in 1890 (and consecrated in 1894). This church seated only about 150 people, however, which proved to be too small for the rapidly growing congregation.

The Automobile Club of Southern California Headquarters, constructed between 1921 and 1923. A striking Spanish Colonial revival building, its courtyard and interior feature artifacts from California's history. In the foreground, one of Los Angeles's first stoplights can be seen. In its early days, the Automobile Club was responsible for installing stoplights, placing road signs and setting speed limits. *Photo courtesy of the University of Southern California archives.*

In 1913, George Davidson (also a USC faculty member) became the rector of St. Johns; in the thirty-eight years he held the job, church membership rose sixfold. It was under Davidson that the decision was made to construct a new, larger church in 1920. Built between 1922 and 1924, and consecrated in 1925, the new St. John's was neo-Romanesque in style, based largely on the eleventh-century St. Peter's Church in Tuscania, Italy. When it opened, it was deemed by the *Los Angeles Times* to be the "most beautiful [church] in Los Angeles."

The church gained notoriety in the 1960s and '70s, when the Reverend E. Lawrence Carter, a social rights activist, held the title of rector. Perhaps the most publicized event occurred in 1970, when Carter symbolically closed the front doors of the cathedral in protest of the Vietnam War; the doors would remain closed until 1973, when the war officially ended. In 2007, St. John's became the procathedral of the Diocese of Los Angeles, with all major services being held there. The building is currently listed on the

The current St. John's Episcopalian Cathedral replaced this wooden, neo-Gothic structure in 1920. The new St. John's, which featured concrete construction and a neo-Romanesque style, was severely needed when it opened in 1925, due to a rapidly increasing congregation. *Photo courtesy of the University of Southern California archives.*

National Register of Historic Places and features many mosaics and stained-glass pieces that have been added over the decades.

JEFFERSON BOULEVARD

The Felix Chevrolet neon sign at the corner of Jefferson Boulevard and Figueroa Street has become a cultural landmark in Los Angeles since its erection in 1958; however, the brand's history with the cartoon cat goes back much further. Felix Chevrolet was first founded in 1921 by Winslow B. Felix, a renowned local car salesman. Shortly after, Felix became friends with Pat Sullivan, creator of the popular comic strip and short film star Felix the Cat. In 1923, in exchange for a new car, Sullivan allowed Felix to use the cat in his advertising. By the end of the silent era, however,

Felix the Cat was quickly forgotten—that is, until 1953, when he made a comeback (this time as a television star). Capitalizing on the success of the show, Felix Chevrolet had the now-famous three-sided sign added when it relocated to its current location in 1958. Recent renovation and a historic landmark status ensure that Felix the Cat will continue to live on for many generations to come.

Arguably the most impressive building in North University Park is the Shrine Auditorium (665 West Jefferson Boulevard), a gigantic Moorish revival theater. In addition to being a performance venue, the building is also the headquarters of the Al Malaikah Temple of Shriners International, a fraternal organization founded on Masonic principles. The Al Malaikah (Los Angeles) chapter of the Shriners was chartered in 1888, initially meeting downtown at Hazard's Pavilion; however, this venue was torn down in 1905, and the Shriners decided to construct their own meeting place. The cornerstone for the original Shrine Auditorium was laid in May 1905, and the building opened to the public the next year. It quickly became a popular venue in Los Angeles, with many organizations utilizing it for gatherings and exhibitions.

The first Shrine Auditorium would not last long, however. On January 11, 1920, the entire structure burned to the ground in only thirty minutes, nearly killing six firefighters in the process. Immediately, though, the organization announced that it planned to rebuild on the same site, after six years of planning and raising the necessary $2.5 million. The two architects on the project—John C. Austin and Abraham M. Edelman—were themselves members of the Al Malaikah Shriners. Austin would go onto design some of Los Angeles's most iconic landmarks, such as city hall and Griffith Observatory. Also a collaborator in the building was G. Albert Lansburgh, who designed the El Capitan and Wiltern Theaters.

Opposite, top: Felix Chevrolet's cartoon sign has been a Los Angeles landmark since it was erected in 1958. Winslow B. Felix, a local car salesman, opened Felix Chevrolet in 1921 and began using the popular cartoon cat as an advertising gimmick in 1923. Recent restoration has brought new life to the sign, ensuring that future generations will be able to appreciate its kitsch.

Opposite, bottom: A very early conceptual drawing of the Shrine Auditorium from the mid-1920s. After the original Shrine Auditorium burned down in 1906, John C. Austin and Abraham M. Edelman were selected to design the new building in a Moorish revival style. Their final design, however, did not include the massive turret featured in this drawing. *Photo courtesy of the Los Angeles Public Library.*

The new Shrine Auditorium opened on January 23, 1926 (with special appearances by silent film legends such as Leatrice Joy and Douglas Fairbanks). The 6,717-seat theater was the largest in the world at that time (and sported the world's largest crystal chandelier, weighing three tons), and an attached exposition hall provided over 100,000 square feet of additional space. Over the years, the Shrine Auditorium has been the host of movie screenings, ballets, sporting events, concerts and countless other events (discussed more in "Visitors to University Park"). Today, the Shrine Auditorium still occupies an entire city block off Jefferson Boulevard, and it is just as impressive in appearance as it was back in 1926. The mosque-inspired onion domes are visible from many of the surrounding areas, and the building serves as a whimsical reminder of the luxury and opulence of the Roaring Twenties.

A more recent addition to North University Park is the University Village Shopping Center, which opened in 1975. Located on Jefferson Boulevard between Hoover and McClintock, University Village provides students with a food court, grocery store and other retail outlets. Also nestled within University Village is Los Angeles Fire Station 15 (915 Jefferson Boulevard), which can trace its roots back to some of the earliest days of the Los Angeles Fire Department. Initially, the station was founded in 1900 as Hose Company No. 4. A wooden Victorian station was built on the small triangle of land that existed between Jefferson Boulevard, McClintock Avenue and Thirty-second Street; due to re-grading of roads, this plot of land no longer exists but would have been on the northwest corner of Jefferson and McClintock (where Cardinal Gardens Apartments currently sits). In 1904, this station was renamed Engine Company No. 15, and the building was expanded and remodeled in a Tudor revival style, complete with a large tower used for drying fire hoses. The station served the university and surrounding areas until 1950, when the current station was opened on July 3. The old fire station existed, boarded up and dilapidating, until the mid-1950s, when the land was converted into a park.

Opposite, top: The Engine Company No. 15 fire station, which was initially constructed in 1900 and remodeled in Tudor revival style in 1904. The building, which sat on the northwest corner of Jefferson Boulevard and McClintock Avenue, served the surrounding community until 1950, when the current fire station opened a block away.

Opposite, bottom: Robert "Red" Manly, the first suspect in the Black Dahlia murder case, inspects Elizabeth Short's handbag and shoes at the University Division Police Station. Short's possessions were discovered shortly after her body was found mutilated in Leimert Park. Manly was able to correctly identify both of her belongings but was later found to be unconnected to her murder. *Photo courtesy of the* Los Angeles Times *archive.*

Located a little more than a block away from the fire station was the first police station constructed in Los Angeles outside of the police department's downtown headquarters. Located at 809 Jefferson Boulevard (the site is now a Denny's restaurant), the University Division Police Station was opened in 1909. For fifty-three years, this station served the surrounding communities, until it was finally decommissioned on February 15, 1962 (when the current station opened about two miles away).

Undoubtedly one of the most memorable events to occur for the police station was the 1947 Black Dahlia murder. On the morning of January 15, Elizabeth Short's body was discovered in a vacant lot less than three and a half miles from the police station. Ten days later, Robert "Red" Manly, the last person to have seen Short alive, was brought into the University Station to identify a woman's shoe and handbag that had been recovered from a dumpster. He correctly identified both the shoe and the purse, claiming he could still smell her perfume on the latter. Manley was quickly acquitted, and the entire case has gone down in history as one of the most famous unsolved murders ever.

Interestingly enough, the Black Dahlia case has another connection to University Park. When Elizabeth Short first moved to California to be with her father in December 1942, she lived in a home located at 1028½ West Thirty-sixth Street, which is where Irani Hall on USC's campus currently stands. Short lived there for only three weeks before moving to Camp Cooke in Lompoc, California.

OTHER NORTH UNIVERSITY PARK LANDMARKS

North University Park is also dotted with many more lesser landmarks, some of which are all but forgotten. The building at 2930 Vermont Avenue now houses a barbershop, bicycle shop and other stores, but it was built in 1912 as the Photoplay silent movie theater (it changed its name to the La Tosca Theater in 1919). From the mid-1950s until its closure in the 1980s, it ran only foreign films. Another movie theater opened on Jefferson between Hoover and McClintock in 1913; called the University Theater, it seated six hundred and catered to students of USC. It was the first theater in Southern California to make its ushers wear uniforms, something that is now commonplace. After being renamed the Realart Theater by 1923 and the Trojan Theater by 1941, it finally closed in December 1952, and the building was razed to make way for University Village.

Another former USC hangout located along Vermont Avenue was a bowling alley called Trojan Bowl. Now Leonardo's Mexican Restaurant, it was opened before 1950 and peaked in popularity in the mid-1970s, before being closed the following decade.

North University Park is also home to the Hebrew Union College's Jack H. Skirball Campus, established in 1954, as well as the USC Caruso Catholic Center. Many USC student housing units are also located nearby, including Century Apartments, Cardinal Gardens and Troy Hall.

North University Park is also home to USC's Fraternity and Sorority Row. Located primarily along West Twenty-eighth Street between Hoover and Figueroa, "The Row" is currently home to twenty-six fraternity houses and nine sorority houses. The first Greek organization to be installed at USC was Kappa Alpha Theta in 1887; it was president George Findley Bovard's wife, Jeanie Allen, who was responsible for founding the chapter. The first male fraternity came only two years later, when Sigma Chi was established at USC. Between 1921 and 1946, seventeen fraternities and nine sororities were established on campus under the direction of president Rufus B. von KleinSmid, and in 1947 and 1948 alone, another seven fraternities were added (due to the large number of young men returning from the war). It was also around this time that fraternities and sororities began to localize along Twenty-eighth Street; many of these original fraternity houses are still in use. Today, Greek life continues to flourish at USC, with about one-fifth of all students being involved.

The future of much of North University Park is very limited; USC currently has plans to demolish University Village, as well as Century Apartments and Cardinal Gardens, in order to build new student housing and a new shopping center. Called The Village at USC, the redevelopment would provide 350,000 square feet of retail space for shops and restaurants, much-needed housing for both undergraduates and graduate students and outdoor space for a farmers' market and special events. While the area will continue to be upgraded and renovated, no amount of construction can erase North University Park's rich history.

Chapter 6

CHESTER PLACE

THE FOUNDING OF CHESTER PLACE

Chester Place is situated north of West Adams Boulevard and west of Figueroa Street. Created in 1899, it was one of the first gated communities in Los Angeles, as well as one of the wealthiest and most opulent neighborhoods in the city. The large mansions that were built by elite citizens at the turn of the twentieth century are now used as the Doheny Campus of Mount St. Mary's College.

Confusingly, Chester Place is the name of two perpendicular streets, as well as being used to refer to the whole neighborhood. The Chester Place that runs north–south between West Adams and Twenty-third Street has been known as Chester Place since 1899, previously having been constructed as a driveway. The second Chester Place runs east–west from St. James Park to Chester Place; this street was formerly known as Twenty-fifth Street and was renamed around 1915.

Although Chester Place technically refers only to the houses located along these two streets, many of the surrounding buildings have histories that are directly linked to the residents of Chester Place and will be discussed in this chapter as well.

The land that would become Chester Place was purchased in 1855 by Henry Hancock, who surveyed much of Los Angeles in the nineteenth century and whose son would have many ties to USC decades later. The tract of land he purchased was very fertile, which, combined with the fact

Nathan Vail's Victorian home, the first house constructed in what would later become the gated community of Chester Place. The home was called Los Pimentos because of pepper trees on the property. Purchased by Judge Charles Silent in 1885, the driveway of the house would become the street that is today known as Chester Place when Silent had the home moved in 1899. *Photo courtesy of the University of Southern California archives.*

An early photo of the West Adams gate to Chester Place (circa 1890s), showing Nathan Vail's home in the background before widespread development of Chester Place. Today, the same gate still stands along West Adams Boulevard. Chester Place was one of the first gated communities in Southern California when it was constructed. *Photo courtesy of the University of Southern California archives.*

that concrete ditches (called "zanjas") brought water from the Los Angeles River to Figueroa and Adams, made the land desirable.

On July 26, 1876, Hancock sold seventeen acres of his land to Nathan Vail, a New Jersey sea captain. Vail built a large, two-story Victorian home on his property, which was located at 711 West Adams and set back from the road behind a large gate made of stone and iron. Today, this gate still stands along West Adams, and what was once the driveway of Vail's home has become the street Chester Place. The home, which was called Los Pimentos because of pepper trees on the property, would have sat approximately where the two Chester Places meet from 1876 to 1899.

Vail sold his home to Judge Charles Silent on November 5, 1885. Silent had moved to Los Angeles after being a federal judge in the Arizona Territory and had entered the real estate business with Nathan Vail. Vail and Silent continued to purchase land in the surrounding areas and even helped to establish towns such as Inglewood and Redondo Beach, until Vail tragically drowned off the coast of Redondo Beach in 1888.

It was in 1899 that Chester Place began to take its current form. Silent decided to move Vail's house north about a block, changing his address to 4 Chester Place. He also extended the original driveway through to Twenty-third Street and subdivided the land on either side. He named this new street after his son, Chester Silent. The street was to be gated and used exclusively by residents of Chester Place. Over the next few years, twelve additional mansions would be built along Chester Place, nine of which are still standing today.

Chester Place's Mansions

Going back to its earliest days, Chester Place was considered "one of the best residential districts in the city" by the *Los Angeles Times*. One of the first homes to be added to Silent's neighborhood was Oliver Posey's house at 8 Chester Place, just south of Vail's relocated home. Undoubtedly the most famous house in the neighborhood, it is now more commonly known as the Doheny Mansion. Oliver Posey had acquired his wealth through a series of gold mines he invested in and moved to California with his wife, Sara, and two sons in 1893. In 1899, Theodore A. Eisen (who would go on to design 2 and 10 Chester Place) and famed Los Angeles architect Sumner P. Hunt designed his Posey's Chester Place mansion. The building's style is hard to

Oliver Posey's ornate mansion at 8 Chester Place. The home, which is an eclectic blend of architectural styles, was purchased by oil magnate Edward L. Doheny in 1901. Doheny and his wife would go on to purchase the rest of the surrounding homes, effectively owning the neighborhood. Today, the house is used by Mount St. Mary's College. *Photo courtesy of the University of Southern California archives.*

describe—it has been referred to as Châteauesque, but it also has elements of Tudor revival, Gothic revival and Mission revival architecture.

Oliver Posey spent much of his time away on business, and on October 24, 1901, he sold his extravagant mansion to Edward L. Doheny for $120,000. Doheny dug his first oil well in Los Angeles in 1892 and is credited with having sparked the Southern California oil boom of the early twentieth century. The Dohenys immediately begun to upgrade the already-stunning twenty-two-room mansion; in about 1905, they purchased (and razed) Nathan Vail's home to the north to provide a larger lawn (today the J. Thomas McCarthy Library sits on the site), and in 1906, they added the Pompeian Room. The Pompeian Room, which replaced a large outdoor patio, is arguably the most famous room in the mansion; it features a twenty-four-foot Tiffany glass dome and colored marble floors. Other rooms in the mansion include the billiards room, a library of rare books and a hunting lodge–style hall. Unlike virtually all of the other Chester Place homes, the interior of the Doheny Mansion is almost perfectly intact and appears much as it has since it was refurbished after the 1933 Long Beach Earthquake.

In 1905, Doheny also constructed the Wigwam Room behind the mansion, complete with shooting range and bowling alley. Other improvements to Chester Place came in the form of a greenhouse, built across the street behind 1 and 7 Chester Place, and a large conservatory, built in 1913 to house the Dohenys' rare plant collection (today, the swimming pool on the property is the sole remnant of the large glass-and-iron building that formerly stood). Estelle Doheny in particular was fond of gardening and hired an entire team of gardeners to maintain the property.

When Edward Doheny purchased Nathan Vail's home in 1905, it set a precedent for what the following decades would be like. Legend has it that it all started after the infamous Teapot Dome Scandal that took place in the early 1920s; Doheny was reportedly so tired of being hounded by the press that he started buying all of the surrounding properties and filling them with friends, family and business associates. His goal was eventually realized, and by the time Estelle Doheny died in 1958, the entire gated community was owned by the Doheny family. Estelle left the neighborhood to the Catholic Archdiocese of Los Angeles in her will, and in 1962 Mount St. Mary's College set up its second campus on the property. Today, the Doheny Mansion is still the focal point of the neighborhood, being used for offices and alumni relations.

Another home that was completed soon after is 10 Chester Place, located on the east side of the street closest to West Adams. This house, built in 1900, was initially owned by William Bayly from Colorado, who bought the property from Silent for $10,000. The home was designed in the Shingle style by Theodore Eisen. One of the more interesting architectural features is the two-story stone gazebo behind the house. Bayly didn't live in his home long, and by 1916 the Doheny family had acquired it, and Ned Doheny (Edward's son) was living there with his family. Ned, his wife and their five children lived at 10 Chester Place until 1928, when they moved into Greystone Mansion in Beverly Hills. Four months later, on February 15, 1929, Ned Doheny and his secretary, Hugh Plunket, would be found dead. Although officially deemed a murder-suicide (due to Plunket suffering a nervous breakdown), many feel that the Doheny family helped cover up Ned's suicide. The next tenant of 10 Chester Place after Ned was USC president Rufus von KleinSmid, who rented the house between 1930 and 1940. The home was later used as a convent for nuns, and today it is the St. Joseph Administration Building at Mount St. Mary's College.

Across the street from 10 Chester Place, on the west side of the road, were originally three houses. Nearest to West Adams was 19 Chester Place, with 17 and 15 Chester Place situated to the north; today, only 17 Chester Place remains. Number 19 Chester Place was originally built in September 1900 by Harry Gray, a grocer. The ten-room mansion featured two-story Roman columns and a third-floor cupola, towering over many of the nearby residences. A little more than a decade later, the house had been demolished to provide 17 Chester Place with a larger lawn; the site remains mostly empty today. A similar fate met 15 Chester Place, which was located on the southwest corner of the two Chester Places. Also built in 1900, it was initially occupied by a real estate investor named B.L. Harding. Designed in the Shingle style (similar to nearby homes), it featured two peaked roofs on the north and a large sloping roof to the south. It changed hands multiple times over the next few decades until it was torn down around 1930, again to make room for 17 Chester Place's lawn. Today, Hannon Residence Hall sits on the site.

Number 17 Chester Place, like its two former neighbors, was constructed in late 1900. Owner Lee W. Foster, like his neighbor to the south, was a grocer. The home was designed by architects A. Wesley Eager and Sumner P. Hunt, the latter of whom also designed 8 and 11 Chester Place, as well as local landmarks such as Casa de Rosas and the Automobile Club Headquarters. Although it appears to be an amalgamation of architectural styles, the architects themselves referred to it as Italian Rennaisance. Foster tragically suffered a stroke on June 5, 1905, and died in the home. Herbert G. Wylie, an employee of Edward Doheny, moved into the house four years later. It was Wylie who was responsible for the destruction of 19 and 15 Chester Place before he sold his home to Doheny in the 1930s. In 1940, USC president Rufus von KleinSmid, who had formerly lived at 10 Chester Place, moved across the street to the larger 17 Chester Place; he stayed in the house after his retirement in 1947 all the way up to his death in 1964. Today, the original home is used as Mount St. Mary's College's Child Development Center.

Three homes located on the east–west Chester Place were not part of Judge Silent's original plot of land; they became part of Chester Place only when the Doheny family acquired them later. The first of these, nearest to the site of 15 Chester Place, is 20 Chester Place. Designed by architect Frank D. Hudson in the Shingle style in 1902, it was initially owned by real estate agent Frederick W. Flint Jr. In 1930, it was sold to the Doheny family, who rented it out to senior oil company employee Frank R. Seaver and his wife, Blanche. Seaver was very philanthropic, and his name can still be seen on the Frank R. Seaver Science Center and Library nearby at USC. Although Frank Seaver passed away in 1964, his wife continued to live at 20 Chester

Place until 1994, when she passed away at the age of 103. Today, the house is still named after the Seavers and serves as office space and student housing. Next door to the Flint house is 22 Chester Place, the Judge Enoch Knight House. Built in a primarily Craftsman style in 1901, Judge Knight lived here until his death on May 16, 1908. After passing through the hands of a surgeon, the Doheny family acquired the house, and it is now used as a home for the Sisters of St. Joseph of Carondelet, who founded Mount St. Mary's College in 1925.

Located across the street from 20 and 22 Chester Place was 21 Chester Place, which predated many of the surrounding houses. Built between 1887 and 1888 for Henry G. Newhall, it was situated between Judge Silent's original property and the nearby St. James Park. By 1896, Henry's brother, Walter S. Newhall, had moved in, and he continued to live there with his wife until his death on Christmas Day 1906. The Doheny family purchased the house in 1915 and rented it out to families for the next half century. Number 21 Chester Place had a brief moment of fame when it was used in the opening credits and first episode of *The Addams Family* in 1964. For subsequent episodes, a painting of the home was used as a backdrop, with artists going as far as to add a third floor and tower to the home. Interestingly, the same year saw the front of the home used as General Scott's (Burt Lancaster) house in *Seven Days in May*. Even after Mount St. Mary's College opened its Doheny Campus and acquired 21 Chester Place, it continued to rent the home out until 1968, after which point it was demolished to make room for Frank D. Lanterman High School. Today, the site of the home is part of the school's track.

North of the intersection of the two Chester Places, there are three houses on the left side of the street: 11, 7 and 1 Chester Place. Number 11 Chester Place, closest to the intersection, was constructed in March 1902 by Sumner P. Hunt and A. Wesley Eager, the team also responsible for 17 Chester Place. The architecture has been described many different ways, but the home is more or less Craftsman style. Artemisia Vermilion, a friend of the Doheny family, lived in the house from the time it was built until her death in 1920. Vermilion also purchased extra lots around the home, giving it a large lawn to the south. In the 1940s, Edward Doheny's sister-in-law was renting the house, and today it is used as a dining hall for students of Mount St. Mary's. On its former south lawn is McIntyre Residence Hall.

Continuing north from 11 Chester Place is 7 Chester Place, one of the most striking homes in the neighborhood. Designed by the noted Los Angeles architectural team of Oliver Perry Dennis and Lyman Farwell in 1903, it features

Artemisia Vermillion's 1902 Craftsman-style home at 11 Chester Place. The mansion was designed by Sumner P. Hunt and A. Wesley Eager, who also designed other houses nearby. Sumner P. Hunt is responsible for many Los Angeles landmarks, including the nearby Automobile Club headquarters and Casa de Rosas. *Photo courtesy of the University of Southern California archives.*

A view looking north at 7 Chester Place, which was constructed in 1903 for Erasmus Wilson. The house, designed by Oliver Perry Dennis and Lyman Farwell, is a classic example of California Mission revival architecture. *Photo courtesy of the University of Southern California archives.*

California Mission revival architecture. Erasmus Wilson and his wife, Flora, lived in the home from 1903 until Erasmus died on August 21, 1920. The house changed hands multiple times but was eventually purchased by the Dohenys and rented to Robert Frank Gross, a mortgage broker, until 1948. Today, the house is used for community services and student housing at the college.

The last home on the west side of the street is 1 Chester Place, originally owned by Austrian count Jaro Von Schmidt and his wife, Elizabeth. This Shingle-style house, built right next to the Twenty-third Street gate into Chester Place, was constructed around 1900. Von Schmidt, a self-described "capitalist," had founded the Bolsa Chica Gun Club in Huntington Beach in 1899. The Dohenys later bought the house and rented it to USC president von KleinSmid's daughter, Betty, and her husband, Ernest Potts. Today, the house has meeting rooms for Mount St. Mary's College, and where there was formerly a large lawn between 1 and 7 Chester Place, there's now a large complex of classrooms, laboratories and the college bookstore.

Also situated near the Twenty-third Street gate, on the eastern side of the street, is 2 Chester Place. Designed by two prominent Los Angeles architects, Theodore Eisen (who designed other mansions in Chester Place) and George Wyman (most famous for the 1893 Bradbury Building downtown), the home is a mix of Tudor revival and Craftsman styles. Dr. William Davis, the original owner, moved into the home in 1902. The house was passed on to the Doheny family in 1930, when they rented it to their attorney, Charles Wellborn. Interestingly, in 1957, Estelle Doheny allowed for Mount St. Mary's College, located in Brentwood, to teach summer courses in this home; it would be only five years until Mount St. Mary's would open an entire satellite campus at Chester Place. Today, 2 Chester Place holds offices for many different educational departments and religious programs.

NEARBY LANDMARKS

The home at 649 West Adams, although not part of Chester Place, still has a very long and interesting history. Captain Rudolph Miner and his wife purchased the home in 1900, after which it fell into the hands of silent movie star Theda Bara. The home, which is now a rectory for priests, is discussed more in depth in the chapter "Film at University Park."

Located at the northwest corner of Figueroa and Adams is St. Vincent de Paul Catholic Church (621 West Adams Boulevard). Although Edward

St. Vincent de Paul Catholic Church, located on the corner of West Adams Boulevard and Figueroa Street, was modeled after an eighteenth-century Mexican church. Opened in 1925, the building was funded by Edward Doheny's wife, Estelle, who was a Roman Catholic. The church was designed by noted Los Angeles architect Albert C. Martin Sr. *Photo courtesy of the Los Angeles Public Library.*

An early drawing of the Stimson House, located on Figueroa Street. The home was constructed in 1891 at a cost of $130,000, making it the most expensive home in Los Angeles at the time. Known as "The Red Castle," the home passed through the hands of a USC fraternity before being purchased by the Doheny family; today, the building is used as a convent.

Doheny was an Episcopalian (and responsible for funding St. John's Church across the street), Estelle Doheny was Roman Catholic and decided to fund the building of a Catholic church near her home. The result was St. Vincent's, which was started in 1923 and opened on April 5, 1925. Designed by Albert C. Martin Sr., who was also responsible for the Million Dollar Theater downtown and the May Company Building on Wilshire, the building features a striking mix of Spanish revival and Churrigueresque architecture.

Martin based his plans for the church off of the Church of Santa Prisca in Taxco, Mexico, built between 1751 and 1758. One of the highlights of St. Vincent's in the forty-five-foot dome, with paintings of the four evangelists inside. The interiors of the church were designed by Ralph Adams Cram, who also designed USC's Doheny Memorial Library, and the interior murals were painted by Sicilian immigrant John B. Smeraldi. The parking lot to the north of the church was formerly the site of Frank Sabichi's mansion. Sabichi was a very important attorney and civil servant in Los Angeles from the 1870s until his death in 1900. Also nearby, to the north of the church, is St. Vincent's School, which was built on its current site in 1954.

Between St. Vincent de Paul Church and St. Vincent's School sits the Stimson House. Although not technically a part of Chester Place, the Stimson House at 2421 Figueroa Street is still a large factor in the history of the neighborhood. Located immediately east of Chester Place, it is the last surviving mansion on Figueroa; formerly, opulent homes lined the street from USC all the way to Bunker Hill downtown. Designed by Los Angeles architect H. Carroll Brown, the home was built in 1891 for Thomas Douglas Stimson, who was a wealthy industrialist, businessman and vice-president of the Los Angeles Chamber of Commerce.

The house, which cost $130,000 to build, was by far the most expensive home in the city at the time. Sandstone was imported from New Mexico to furnish the outside of the thirty-room home, which features a four-story tower, brick chimneys and battlements along the rooftop (earning the building its nickname: "The Red Castle"). This home is by far the finest example of Richardson Romanesque architecture left in Los Angeles. Although the style was popular nationally in the 1890s, it never became prominent in Southern California. Many features, including the tower, also bear a strong resemblance to Victorian Gothic architecture. The inside of the house is no less impressive than the exterior; each room on the lower floor was constructed with a different type of wood paneling, including mahogany, walnut and oak. The house also features stained-glass windows and a full basement, complete with wine cellar.

A bizarre attack on the mansion took place in February 1896. An employee of Stimson, Harry Coyne, lit a stick of dynamite against the foundation of the house. Had the building been constructed of wood, it would have been destroyed completely, but the mansion's thick stone walls resisted the blast, and damage was minimal. Coyne was caught and sentenced to five years in Folsom Prison. Thomas Stimson got to enjoy his mansion for only a few more years, until his death in 1898; his wife continued to live there until 1904. An engineer, Alfred Solano, and a brewer, Edward Maier, were the next two owners of the home, until 1940, when Maier sold the home to USC's Pi Kappa Alpha fraternity for $20,000.

Within a year, the Stimson House was home to one of the most infamous events in Trojan history. On November 8, 1940, UCLA students lit the annual USC bonfire at the Kappa Alpha Theta house hours before it was supposed to take place. Eight hundred USC students quickly began rioting along Twenty-eighth Street, burning everything from sticks to wooden benches. Over thirty policemen and firemen had to use physical force to break up the students, who formed a wall of resistance. Two of the UCLA culprits, including the son of the Los Angeles chief of police, were captured and held hostage in the basement of the Stimson House. After shaving their heads, stripping them of their clothes and painting "SC" on their chests, the students were brought to campus in a cage and exhibited on stage. After an apology was issued by UCLA, which offered to pay $200 for the cost of the bonfire, USC president von KleinSmid suggested the money be donated to charity.

To rid herself of the constant fraternity parties, Estelle Doheny purchased the home from Pi Kappa Alpha in 1948 for $75,000. The home became a convent for the Sisters of St. Joseph until 1969, when the Stimson House began being used as housing for Mount St. Mary's College. In 1993, the Sisters of St. Joseph returned, and the building is still in use as a convent today. In 1994, the home suffered considerable damage in the Northridge Earthquake, but fortunately extensive reconstruction retained the architectural integrity of the building. The house can still be seen from Figueroa, the last reminder of the dozens of mansions that once lined the street.

A discussion on Chester Place isn't complete without a mention of the nearby St. James Park. Around the time that Chester Place was being developed, the St. James Park area (immediately to the west) was also becoming one of the wealthiest neighborhoods in the city. Initially, the land was owned by J. Downey Harvey (whose uncle was USC co-founder and ex-governor John G. Downey); in 1887, Harvey subdivided the land around a central private park (the namesake of the neighborhood). Today, the small park still exists intact, situated in one of the most concentrated historic and architecturally significant neighborhoods in Los Angeles. The National Register of Historic Places recognizes ninety buildings within the St. James Park Historic District, with many fine examples of Eastlake and Queen Anne Victorian, Craftsman, Colonial revival and Classical revival homes.

Today, Chester Place is one of Los Angeles's underappreciated gems. It is an oasis surrounded by the hustle and bustle of city life, still very much the same as it was when inhabited by some of the most significant figures in the city. Fortunately, Mount St. Mary's College has done an excellent job of preserving the neighborhood's legacy and integrity, and it will hopefully be around for generations to come.

Chapter 7

SPORTS AT UNIVERSITY PARK

USC TROJAN FOOTBALL

Few schools in the nation can claim the same number of athletic achievements as the University of Southern California. Collectively, the university has won 118 team national championships (including 96 NCAA titles) as of 2012, which is the third most of any university behind UCLA and Stanford.

Undoubtedly, the most well-known part of USC's athletic legacy is its football program. With eleven national championships, six Heisman Trophy winners and an all-time winning percentage over 70 percent, USC's football team is one of the most historic and prestigious in the nation. USC's first football team came together in 1888, less than a decade after the school was founded. On November 14 of that year, it defeated the Alliance Athletic Club 16–0 in its first game ever.

The first two coaches were Frank Suffel and Henry Goddard; the team would play without a coach for the next eight years. The first USC quarterback, Arthur Carroll, sewed the pants for the first team himself. He would go on to become a tailor later in life. In the early years, USC played only two or three games a year, sometimes not even playing an entire season. Its first game against another college was a win over St. Vincent's in 1889. Other regular opponents included Throop College (later Cal Tech), Occidental College, Whittier College, Loyola College, Pomona College and Los Angeles High School.

The football program began to pick up speed by the turn of the century, and by 1903, USC was playing a longer season with more diverse opponents.

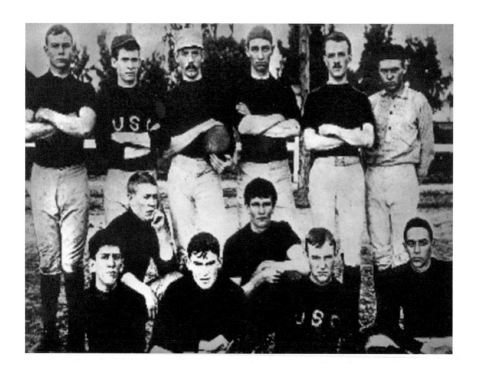

Perhaps the only known photograph of USC's first football team in 1888. This team defeated the Alliance Athletic Club 16–0 in its first game ever that year. In the early years of the program, USC's football team would sometimes play only two or three games per season. It wasn't until the 1920s that the team would come into national prominence.

In 1904, Harvey Holmes became the first paid football coach, in addition to coaching track and baseball. November 4, 1905, was a day of firsts for USC: it was the first game it played outside Southern California, its first game against a major university and the beginning of its longest-standing rivalry (with Stanford). USC was by no means prepared to play such a powerhouse, as evidenced by its 16–0 loss.

In 1909, a very important figure in USC took over as head coach: Dean Cromwell, who would (more famously) also become the USC track coach that same year. Cromwell had officiated USC football games going back to 1903, and his connections to the school would continue until his retirement in 1948. USC's football team disbanded for three seasons between 1911 and 1913 in favor of a rugby team (a popular trend at the time). Football was reinstated in 1914 and was coached for two years by Ralph Glaze.

Cromwell again took over in 1916, but soon after, World War I caused a shortage of young men, and the team suffered greatly. Further trouble was caused by the Spanish influenza of 1918, which prevented any games from being played in Los Angeles for most of the season. USC's next coach, Gus Henderson, lasted six seasons, until 1924. It was under Henderson that USC won its first bowl game—the 1922 Rose Bowl against Penn State.

By the early 1920s, Los Angeles's population was increasing exponentially. In 1880, when USC was founded, the city had just 11,200 people; by 1920, the population had increased more then fiftyfold to 576,700 people. Up until this point, USC's home football games had been played off campus. The vast majority of games through 1917 were played at Fiesta Park (bordered by Pico Boulevard, Grand Avenue, Twelfth Street and Hope Street), with the exception of the 1903 season, which was played at Prager Park (located at Grand Avenue and Washington Boulevard). From 1918 until 1922, USC played its football games at the original Bovard Field, which was located behind the Old College building, where USC's music school is currently located.

It became apparent that a large, outdoor venue was a necessity for the city, so following the close of World War I, the Los Angeles Memorial Coliseum was commissioned as a tribute to veterans. It was designed by the prolific Los Angeles architectural team of John and Donald Parkinson, who were also responsible for many of the historic buildings on USC's campus. A combination of ancient Greco-Roman architecture and contemporary Art Deco, ground was broken for the Coliseum on December 21, 1921. The stadium opened, on schedule, less than a year and a half later, on May 1, 1923. Construction costs were just shy of $1 million, and the stadium initially seated about seventy-five thousand people (making it the largest stadium in Los Angeles).

USC's connections to the Coliseum can be traced back to the building's earliest days. When determining where to build a stadium in Los Angeles, USC said that if a stadium were built in Exposition Park, it would play all of its home games there. It was taken up on the offer, and the first football game to be held at the Coliseum was on October 6, 1923, between USC and Pomona College (USC won 23–7). The following season, the Coliseum was the site of the Los Angeles Christmas Festival bowl game between USC and the University of Missouri. In 1928, the Trojans were joined at the Coliseum by their cross-town rivals, the UCLA Bruins. The Bruins would share the Coliseum between 1928 and 1981, when they moved to the Pasadena Rose Bowl. During these years, USC and UCLA would alternate being the home team when they played each other.

USC first came into the national spotlight in the early 1920s, led by coach "Gloomy Gus" Henderson. In 1925, Howard Jones replaced Henderson,

The Los Angeles Memorial Coliseum, constructed between 1921 and 1923, is one of the most storied venues in sporting history. Home to USC's football games, the venue has also seen two Olympic Games, a World Series, two Super Bowls and countless other events. The unique blend of Art Deco and Greco-Roman architecture was designed by John and Donald Parkinson. *Photo courtesy of the University of Southern California archives.*

and USC continued to become a dominant force in the college football world. Over the sixteen years that Jones was coach, USC won its first four national championships in 1928, 1931, 1932 an 1939. He also won all five Rose Bowl games in which he coached USC. Jones, one of the most legendary college football coaches in history, tragically died of a heart attack in 1941 at the age of only fifty-five; he was inducted into the College Football Hall of Fame in 1951. USC's practice football field on campus is called the Howard Jones Field in his honor.

Over the next two decades, USC would never recapture its success under Howard Jones. Led by Sam Barry (1941), Jeff Cravath (1942–50), Jess Hill (1951–56) and Don Clark (1957–59), USC would still manage to capture six Rose Bowls (1943, 1944, 1945, 1947, 1952 and 1954) without any national championships.

Coach John McKay, nicknamed the "Silver Fox," stands with his undefeated 1972 Trojan team on the field of the Coliseum. During McKay's sixteen years as head coach, he won four national championships and five Rose Bowls. His 1970s teams are considered some of the best college football teams in history. *Photo courtesy of the Los Angeles Public Library.*

In 1960, the man who will forever be most associated with USC football became head coach. One of Don Clark's assistant coaches in 1959, John McKay, was hired as a replacement after Clark's resignation. McKay, who would coach USC until 1975, before coaching in the NFL, led his teams to four national championships in 1962, 1967, 1972 and 1974. He also coached two Heisman Trophy winners: Mike Garrett in 1965 and O.J. Simpson in 1968. He remains the winningest coach in USC football history.

Since McKay, USC has won three national championships—in 1978 under John Robinson and in 2003 and 2004 under Pete Carroll. Heisman Trophies have also been awarded to Charles White (1979), Marcus Allen (1981), Carson Palmer (2002), Matt Leinart (2004) and Reggie Bush (2005).

The Los Angeles Memorial Coliseum

In addition to hundreds of USC football games, the Coliseum has an extremely diverse sports history. The Coliseum experienced a large rise in importance when it was decided in 1923 that the 1932 Summer Olympics would be held in Los Angeles. In preparation, the Parkinsons renovated and added to the Coliseum in 1930.

The 1932 Olympics are interesting for a number of reasons. Due to the Great Depression, fewer than half of the participatory nations in the 1928 Olympics were able to afford the trip to California; not even President Herbert Hoover attended the games. However, the games resulted in approximately $1 million in profit for the City of Los Angeles. The 1932 games were also the first to feature an Olympic Village (located in Baldwin Hills), and Tenth Street was renamed Olympic Boulevard due to the fact that it was the Tenth Modern Olympic Games.

Many of the game's events were held in Exposition Park. In addition to hosting the opening and closing ceremonies, the Coliseum (called Olympic Stadium in 1932) held the track and field events, equestrian events, field hockey and gymnastics. Fencing was held at the State Armory Building, while the art competitions were held at the Natural History Museum.

The swimming, water polo and diving events were held at the Los Angeles Swimming Stadium. An Art Deco masterpiece, the stadium was recently renovated in 2002 and 2003 and was renamed the LA84 Foundation/John C. Argue Swim Stadium. John C. Argue was a lawyer who was largely responsible for bringing the Olympic Games back to Los Angeles in 1984.

Opposite, top: An aerial view of the opening ceremonies of the 1932 Olympic Games. In preparation for the games, the Parkinsons renovated the stadium and added thousands of seats. However, the Great Depression caused many nations to withdraw, making it one of the smallest Modern Olympics. Behind the Coliseum, the newly constructed Los Angeles Swimming Stadium can be seen. *Photo courtesy of the Los Angeles Public Library.*

Opposite, bottom: The closing ceremonies of the 1984 Olympic Games at the Coliseum. For these games, USC's campus was converted into an Olympic Village. During both the 1932 and 1984 Olympics, track and field events were held at the Coliseum, with other events being held at other Southern California venues. *Photo courtesy of the Los Angeles Public Library.*

The 1984 Olympic Games were also held at the Coliseum, making it the only building in the world to host two Olympic games. Opened by President Ronald Reagan, the 1984 games featured a record 140 participating nations, despite a boycott by the Soviet Union and allied nations. As with the 1932 Olympics, the opening and closing ceremonies (as well as track and field events) were held at the Coliseum; boxing was held at the Los Angeles Memorial Sports Arena, and other events were held across Southern California. The Olympic Village sat on USC's campus, with Marianne & J. Douglas Pardee Tower (now an undergraduate residence hall) being constructed to house athletes.

Outside of the Olympics, the building was also the home of the Los Angeles Rams of the National Football League from 1946 until 1980, when they relocated to Anaheim. From 1982 to 1994, the Oakland Raiders moved to Los Angeles and used the stadium as well. The stadium was also the site of the 1967 and 1973 Super Bowls.

In addition to these two NFL teams, the Coliseum was also the home of the Los Angeles Dons of the All-America Football Conference played at the Coliseum from 1946 to 1949 and the Los Angeles Chargers of the American Football League in 1960 before relocating to San Diego. Other professional football teams to play at the Coliseum were the Los Angeles Express of the United States Football League from 1983 to 1985 and the Los Angeles Xtreme of the XFL in 2001.

Despite the building's oval shape, the Coliseum was also utilized as a baseball stadium for a brief period. The Los Angeles Dodgers, having just moved from Brooklyn, played at the Coliseum from 1958 to 1961 while Dodger Stadium was being constructed. Due to the strange dimensions of the field, the left-field fence was only 251 feet from home plate. In 1959, three games of the World Series between the Dodgers and the Chicago White Sox were held at the Coliseum; the crowd of 92,706 fans at each game is still a World Series record for attendance. The 1959 MLB All-Star Game was also held at the Coliseum.

USC TROJAN BASEBALL

Another of the more legendary athletic programs at USC is its baseball team. Having won twelve national championships and thirty-eight conference championships as of this writing, they are considered by some to be the most prestigious college baseball program in history. Legends such as Fred Lynn, Tom Seaver, Mark McGuire and Randy Johnson all played for the Trojans before rising to fame.

USC's baseball program began in 1889, when on November 23 they lost to a team known as Bonny Brae by a score of 13–10. The first few decades of USC baseball, however, were plagued by inconsistent management and scheduling. As a whole, though, Trojan baseball teams performed fairly well, and highlights included a coaching stint by Hall of Fame pitcher Rube Waddell in 1902 and USC's first international baseball game against Japan in 1905. It was also around this time that USC's baseball team had the first batting cage on the West Coast.

In 1924, baseball legend Sam Crawford took over as head coach. "Wahoo Sam," who played Major League Baseball for nineteen seasons, is best remembered as a slugger for the Detroit Tigers in the first decades of the twentieth century. He still holds the record for most career triples, with 309, and is consistently ranked amongst the greatest hitters of all time. While coaching at USC, Crawford helped to establish the California Intercollegiate Baseball Association, the league in which USC competed until its dissolution in 1966.

After six years of Crawford's leadership, Sam Barry picked up where he left off, taking charge of USC baseball in 1930. Barry had previously been an assistant football coach at the University of Iowa under Howard Jones. In 1929, Jones, now the coach of the Trojan football team, hired Barry again as an assistant. Jones also became the coach of USC's basketball team that same year, and the following season he began coaching baseball.

Sam Barry became an important figure in USC history. In 1941, he simultaneously was the head coach for football, baseball and basketball (the only man to do such), and he is one of only three people in history to lead a basketball team to the Final Four and a baseball team to the College World Series. Within his first decade, Barry led USC to five division titles.

In 1942, the name most often associated with USC baseball began his tenure as head coach. Rod Dedeaux was born in New Orleans on February 17, 1914. He attended Hollywood High School and USC and ended up playing two games for the Brooklyn Dodgers in 1935. However, he soon decided to focus on coaching. In 1942, Sam Barry, under whom Dedeaux had played during his college days, offered Dedeaux a job as co–head coach. Barry would leave to serve in the navy during World War II, leaving Dedeaux as the sole head coach for three seasons. Upon Barry's return in 1946, USC's baseball program began to transform into a powerhouse for the first time. Under Dedeaux and Barry, USC managed to win the second-ever College World Series in 1947, taking two out of three games from a Yale team led by George H.W. Bush.

On September 23, 1950, Sam Barry passed away, leaving Dedeaux the sole coach of USC's baseball team. Beginning with the 1951 season, USC would win eleven straight CIBA titles, making it one of the strongest college baseball programs in the nation. USC would claim its second College World Series title in 1958, defeating Missouri in the finals. Further College World Series titles under Dedeaux would come in 1961, 1963, 1968, 1970, 1971, 1972, 1973, 1974 and 1978—more than any other school in the

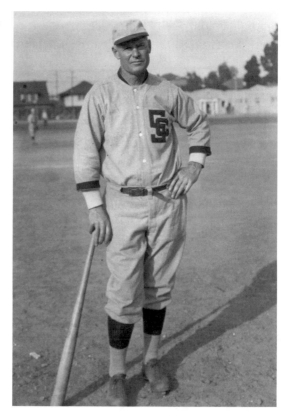

"Wahoo Sam" Crawford, still considered one of the greatest hitters in baseball history, served as the coach of USC baseball from 1924 to 1929. Crawford, a member of the National Baseball Hall of Fame, still holds the record for most career triples. Crawford also helped to establish the California Intercollegiate Baseball Association. *Photo courtesy of the University of Southern California archives.*

country. Until his retirement in 1986, Dedeaux was the winningest coach in college baseball history, with an overall record of 1,332-571-11.

Beginning in the program's earliest days, USC played its baseball games at Bovard Field, where the football team had played until the Coliseum was built. Home plate was located between Bovard Administration Building and the Annenberg School for Communication; a plaque still marks the site of the left field line. In use until 1973, Bovard Field saw many historic games. However, perhaps none is as memorable as the exhibition game that was played on March 26, 1951, between the USC Trojans and the New York Yankees. It was the only time that the Yankees ever trained on the West

Dedeaux Field has been the home of Trojan baseball since 1974. The stadium is named after Rod Dedeaux, USC's baseball coach from 1950 to 1986, who is considered by many to be the greatest college baseball coach ever. He led USC to ten College World Series titles and is still the winningest coach in college baseball history.

Coast, as well as the only time a major-league team played a college team on a college campus. The Yankees, who had just won two consecutive World Series, brought along a star nineteen-year-old rookie by the name of Mickey Mantle. Mantle hit two home runs that day, including one that was estimated to have traveled 656 feet—which would make it the second longest of his career. While the homer's actual length has become shrouded in myth and legend, what is undeniable is that Mantle—and one of the most powerful Yankees teams in history—shared the field with the most dominant college baseball program of all time.

Despite offers from major-league teams (including the Dodgers) to coach in the MLB, Rod Dedeaux always refused, stating that he preferred the college game. During his tenure as coach, he took a salary of only one dollar, using his other businesses to support himself. Other notable achievements of Dedeaux include coaching the 1964 and 1984 Olympic baseball teams, induction to the American Baseball Coaches Hall of Fame in 1970 and the College Baseball Hall of Fame in 2006 and the title of "Coach of the Century" from *Collegiate Baseball* magazine. Dedeaux passed away at the age of ninety-one on January 5, 2006, of complications from a stroke. His legacy lives on at USC's campus in the form of Dedeaux Field, the home of USC baseball since 1974.

USC Trojan Basketball and the Sports Arena

USC's basketball program can be traced back to 1907, when Emil Breitkreutz (the first Trojan ever to compete in the Olympic games) was head coach. Dean Cromwell, of track and field fame, coached the team in a two-game season in 1918. But by the 1920s, USC had become a dominant force and was widely considered to be the best team in Southern California, winning its first league title in 1928. Sam Barry, also USC's baseball and football coach, took over in 1929, leading the team to eight division titles in ten years. Another highlight came during the 1930s and early '40s, when USC won forty-two consecutive games against cross-town rivals the UCLA Bruins.

It was in 1940 that USC basketball had its heyday. USC was considered the nation's greatest college basketball team, but it was upset at the buzzer in a semifinal game against Kansas. Throughout the following decades, USC continued to have a strong basketball program, making it to the Final Four a second time in 1954. The team has also had brief periods of resurgence in more recent years, qualifying for the NCAA tournament seven times between 1997 and 2011.

USC played many basketball games up through the 1940s on the stage of the Shrine Auditorium, making for a very strange viewing situation for the fans. In 1949, the team moved across town to the Pan-Pacific Auditorium in the Fairfax District. The team returned to University Park in 1959, however, when the Los Angeles Memorial Sports Arena was constructed.

The Los Angeles Memorial Sports Arena, located adjacent to the Coliseum, opened on July 4, 1959, with a celebration featuring Vice President Richard Nixon. In addition to being the home of Trojans basketball from 1959 until 2006, it has also been the home of countless other sporting events. USC's cross-town rivals, the UCLA Bruins, shared the court from 1959 until 1965 and again returned to play the 2011–12 season while their own Pauley Pavilion was undergoing a refurbishment.

Other sports teams that have called the building home include the National Basketball Association's Los Angeles Lakers (1960–67) and Los Angeles Clippers (1984–99), the American Basketball Association's Los Angeles Stars (1968–70), the Western Hockey League's Los Angeles Blades

The Los Angeles Memorial Sports Arena was constructed adjacent to the Coliseum in 1959. For many years, the arena was home to USC's basketball team, in addition to the Los Angeles Lakers and Clippers basketball teams, the Los Angeles Kings hockey team and numerous other professional sports teams. Vice President Richard Nixon spoke at the building's dedication. *Photo courtesy of the Los Angeles Public Library.*

(1961–67), the National Hockey League's Los Angeles Kings (1967), the World Hockey Association's Los Angeles Sharks (1972–74) and the Arena Football League's Los Angeles Cobras (1988).

Numerous other significant sporting events have also been held in the building. The 1963 NBA All-Star Game, featuring legends such as Bill Russell and Wilt Chamberlain, was held at the Sports Arena, as were the 1968 and 1972 NCAA Final Four games. In addition, the 1984 Olympics, based at the Coliseum, held its boxing events inside the Sports Arena. Throughout the late 1980s and early '90s, many wrestling events took place there, including the 1994 "When Worlds Collide" fight, which is credited with having introduced Americans to Mexican *lucha libre* wrestling.

Plans for a new USC arena began in 2002, when Louis and Helene Galen donated $10 million for such a building (eventually, their contributions would total $50 million). The groundbreaking ceremony for the Galen Center was held on October 31, 2004. In addition to being the home of USC basketball, the building also houses USC's volleyball games, which were previously held in the North Gym inside the Physical Education Building.

Other USC Trojan Sports

One of the most fondly remembered names in USC sports history is Dean Cromwell. Already mentioned briefly as one of USC's early football coaches, he was born in Turner, Oregon, in 1879 and attended Occidental College, where he played many sports. He began coaching USC's track and field team in 1909, the same year he began coaching football. In the forty years that he coached USC, he led USC's outdoor track and field team to twelve NCAA championships (the team has gone on to win fourteen more in the years since Cromwell).

One of Cromwell's athletes, Jess Mortensen (who was captain of the 1930 team), became USC's coach in 1951 and won seven NCAA titles in his eleven years. Over the years, sixty USC track and field athletes have won medals in the Olympic Games, and sixty-one Trojans have equaled or bettered track and field world records, making USC's program one of the most storied in the nation. Today, USC's track field is still called Cromwell Field in memory of the team's first great leader.

Although not as prominent as football or baseball, USC's tennis team has a long and storied history. The most legendary figure in the program's history is undoubtedly George Toley, who served as head coach from 1954 to 1980 and is a member of the Intercollegiate Tennis Hall of Fame. Toley, who was himself a USC graduate in 1942, led the team to ten NCAA team championships and had a career winning percentage of 82.1 percent.

Upon Toley's retirement in 1980, one of his former All-American players, Dick Leach, took over the program. Under Leach, the Trojans managed to win another three national titles. The most recent USC tennis coach, who took over in 2003, is Peter Smith, who led the team to four consecutive national championships from 2009 to 2012.

In USC's earliest days, tennis courts were located near the original university building, near the current site of Annenberg School for Communications. However, with the development of Bovard Field, these courts were removed shortly after the school was founded. Since at least the early 1930s, tennis courts were located adjacent to the original cinema (formerly architecture) building; these courts were removed when Leavy Library was constructed in 1993. In the 1950s, another set of courts was located where Heritage Hall stands today. However, since 1973, the home of USC tennis has been the David X. Marks Tennis Stadium, located on the west side of campus adjacent to Vermont Avenue. The site of the 1974 NCAA championship, the stadium is named for David X. Marks, a World War I pilot and generous benefactor to USC (he is also memorialized by Marks Hall and Marks Tower residence halls on campus).

USC's swimming program was established in 1929 and has consistently been an extremely strong force in the collegiate swimming world. USC swimmers have earned seventy-nine Olympic medals, including thirty-eight gold. But the name most often associated with the program, Peter Daland, began his tenure as head coach in 1957. Daland, who also coached the U.S. Women's Olympic swim team in 1964 and the men's team (including Mark Spitz) in 1972, led USC to all nine of its NCAA championships and had a winning percentage of almost 92 percent during his thirty-five years as coach. Daland is also the only swimming coach in history to have won an NCAA title, a men's Amateur Athletic Union title (which he did fourteen times) and a women's Amateur Athletic Union title (which he did twice). Daland retired from his position in 1992 and was succeeded by another former Olympic coach, Mark Schubert, who would go on to coach the U.S. National team.

Early maps of USC show a pool near the old men's gymnasium, approximately where Mudd Hall of Philosophy sits today. The Physical Education building, opened in 1930, includes an indoor pool that can still be used by students today. With the coming of the Olympic Games to Los Angeles in 1984, McDonald's restaurants provided funding for a new swim stadium, located on USC's campus. Opened in 1983, the complex was used for swimming, diving and synchronized swimming during the Olympics, as well as many competitions since. On November 2, 2012, ground was broken for the new, multimillion-dollar Uytengsu Aquatics Center and Peter Daland Pool, featuring state-of-the-art facilities for swimmers and seating for 1,500 spectators.

Many apocryphal stories surround the genesis of the name "the Trojans." Many people know it was first used by *Los Angeles Times* reporter Owen R. Bird in 1912; few people, however, know the circumstances behind its initial usage. Bird, who was a prominent sportswriter during the early 1900s, first used the term in the February 24, 1912 issue of the *Los Angeles Times*. Many fans assume that the nickname was given to the USC football team, but Bird actually applied it to the USC track team after a meet against Occidental College. School nicknames were popular during that time, and USC (which had formerly been called the Methodists or Wesleyans) decided that the rebranding was a welcome change.

In reflecting on the name he bestowed on the underdog USC track team, Bird stated that "the term 'Trojan' as applied to USC means to me that no matter what the situation, what the odds or what the conditions, the competition must be carried on to the end and those who strive must give all they have and never be weary in doing so." In 2012, USC celebrated the 100th anniversary of its moniker, which embodies the spirit and determination that USC athletes have carried on for over a century.

To celebrate USC's athletic history, the university constructed Heritage Hall, a three-story building designed to house the Athletic Department and showcase the university's trophies and achievements. Ground was broken on the $2.8 million structure on February 5, 1970, and the building opened to the public the following year. Expansions came in 1984, 1992 and 1998, and in 2013, a major renovation of the building began. Also adding to USC's athletic facilities is the John McKay Center, a $70 million complex that opened on August 21, 2012.

Chapter 8

FILM AT UNIVERSITY PARK

EARLY FILMS

The University of Southern California is deeply rooted in the film history of Los Angeles. Dating back to the mid-1920s, literally hundreds of movies and television shows have been filmed in University Park, utilizing locations such as the Exposition Park museums and the historic core of USC's campus. Shortly after movies began to be filmed in University Park, the USC School of Cinematic Arts was founded in 1929, further strengthening the ties between USC and Hollywood. Today, the campus and surrounding areas are still used frequently for shoots, and the film school at USC is consistently ranked among the top in the country and the world.

Some of the earliest films shot in the area were the silent films of Buster Keaton and Harold Lloyd. The stately brick buildings at both USC and Exposition Park provided striking backgrounds for many early movies. Other factors that brought moviemakers to University Park were the large athletic facilities (both the Los Angeles Memorial Coliseum and Bovard Field at USC were used frequently), as well as the convenience of having a streetcar that ran right through the heart of campus (which was used more than once as a prop).

Probably the earliest movie to be shot at University Park was Buster Keaton's 1922 short film, *Cops*. In the movie, Keaton plays a down-on-his-luck young man who has constant run-ins with the law, despite his good intentions. While being chased by police, Keaton is cornered against the odd, wedge-shaped College of Dentistry Building, which was located on Exposition Boulevard and Thirty-sixth Place until its demolition in 1972. Keaton again used the same building in 1925's *Seven Chances*. In this film, Keaton finds out on his twenty-seventh birthday that he has inherited a huge fortune, but he can only claim it if he is married by seven o'clock that night. After failing to propose to his girlfriend, as well as seven other women he attempts to win over, he places an advertisement in the paper to find a prospective bride. At the appointed time, hundreds of women arrive at the church and proceed to chase Keaton through the streets of Los Angeles. A brief shot during the chase scene shows Keaton and his pursuers running east on Exposition Boulevard, past the same dentistry building that he had used three years prior. In the same chase scene, Bovard Auditorium makes a brief cameo (as it does in the 1923 Harold Lloyd film *Safety Last*).

Other silent movies film at University Park are Harold Lloyd's *The Freshman* (1925) and Buster Keaton's *College* (1927). Both tell the story of young college students struggling to fit in—Lloyd trying to become popular on the football team and Keaton trying to impress the girl he loves by becoming a jock—and both movies were shot at many of the same locations. Each of the films features shots in Exposition Park in front of the Natural History Museum and the State Exposition Building, which were used as stand-ins for collegiate buildings. There are also athletic sequences in both movies shot at USC's former Bovard Field, as well as a track scene shot at the Los Angeles Memorial Coliseum. Keaton would return to the Natural History Museum for a brief shot in his 1929 movie *Spite Marriage*.

When Buster Keaton was filming in University Park in the 1920s, he was no stranger to the area. In March 1919, an up-and-coming Keaton had moved into the home on 649 West Adams Boulevard with the most famous comedic actor on the planet, Roscoe "Fatty" Arbuckle. The house itself has a past steeped in cinematic history. Built in 1905, the house was the home of famed silent film actress Theda Bara at the peak of her popularity in the late 1910s. Much to the chagrin of her neighbors, Bara, nicknamed "The Vamp," brought much of her raucous lifestyle to what had formerly been a quiet neighborhood. Living up to her mysterious movie persona, she filled the house with tiger-skin rugs, crystal balls and sarcophagi. However, her popularity began to decline shortly thereafter, and by 1918, she was married and living in Beverly Hills. Over the next few months, the house was rented by Russian silent film star Alla Nazimova.

If the surrounding homes were looking for peace and quiet after Theda Bara's departure, however, they must have been severely disappointed when Fatty Arbuckle (an even more boisterous figure than Bara) moved in the next year. If the quarter-million-dollar price tag for the house wasn't enough, Arbuckle bought such luxuries as a $15,000 front door and a $75,000 Chinese rug. The garage held six cars, including Roscoe's custom $25,000 Pierce Arrow, which even had a full bar and toilet in the backseat. He held frequent all-night parties, sometimes with a complete orchestra and hundreds of guests. Allegedly, Edward L. Doheny Sr. found the drunken guests and loud noises so bothersome that he would walk from his home on Chester Place during the night to knock on Arbuckle's door and offer him any amount of money for the house, just to rid himself of the nuisance.

When Keaton moved in with Arbuckle, the home became the site of one of the most famous practical jokes in Hollywood history. Arbuckle held a dinner party for famed studio executive Adolph Zukor, who was making his annual trip to Los Angeles; also in attendance were such early Hollywood legends

Silent film comedian Roscoe "Fatty" Arbuckle poses with his custom $25,000 Pierce Arrow in front of his West Adams home. Arbuckle, well known for his excessive opulence, had a full bar and toilet installed in the back of the car. While living in this home, an up-and-coming young actor named Buster Keaton would often live with him.

as Sid Grauman, Bebe Daniels and Alice Lake. Keaton, who was still not widely recognizable, was to play the butler and waiter that evening. Arbuckle let everyone except for Zukor in on the elaborate setup. During dinner, Keaton performed such stunts as spilling soup all over himself and pouring cold water into Arbuckle's lap. The climax of the night came when Keaton carried out a twenty-pound turkey, reached over to pick a napkin up off the floor, and was hit from behind with the swinging kitchen door, sending the turkey flying across the room. Arbuckle, in a false fit of rage, broke a prop bottle over Keaton's head and chased him out onto Adams Boulevard. The ultimate payoff came when, once everything had settled down, Keaton (having changed his clothes) phoned Arbuckle to say he'd be joining them for dessert. Zukor was excited, having heard a lot about the rising star, but when he recognized Keaton, all he could say was "Very clever, boys."

In 1921, tragedy struck for Arbuckle when he was accused of the rape and murder of Virginia Rappe. In 1923, he rented the home to director Raoul Walsh and actress Miriam Cooper. Only a year later, Joseph Schenck (Arbuckle's former producer) moved in with his esteemed wife, Norma Talmadge. Schenck and Talmadge moved out in the mid-1920s, thus ending the unforgettable Hollywood legacy of 649 West Adams.

Another supposed Hollywood scandal from this era has connections to USC. In 1965, Kenneth Anger published the now-infamous *Hollywood Babylon*, in which he allegedly detailed the most salacious scandals in Hollywood up to that time. One story that instantly caught on was that Clara Bow, the most famous actress of the late-1920s, was intimate with the entire USC football team. To fans, this story did not seem out of the question—Bow's scandalous social life was well documented during her lifetime. However, the USC story has been debunked time and time again. While Clara Bow did attend USC football games in 1926 and 1927, and even went on a date with the quarterback, Morley Drury, the stories Anger published have no basis in fact. What actually happened is that Bow became so fascinated by USC football that she began holding parties after each game for the team; however, Bow's father did not approve of these parties, and no alcohol was even permitted (let alone the kinds of mischief that Anger claims). One USC football player even confessed, "We had a good time, but it wasn't that exciting."

It was also around this time that one of the most famous actresses ever, Greta Garbo, would visit USC for a publicity photo shoot. In early 1926, Garbo, still a twenty-year-old starlet, was asked to pose with USC's track and field team. Garbo initially refused; however, MGM quickly deducted twenty-

Greta Garbo poses with a USC track coach in 1926 as part of a publicity stunt. Garbo initially rejected the idea of posing with the university's track team but quickly reconsidered when MGM deducted twenty-five dollars from her salary. Garbo was only twenty years old when the photos were taken.

five dollars from her salary, and she quickly reconsidered. Photographer Don Gillum noted how unhappy Garbo looked during the shoot.

In 1930, the comedic duo of Stan Laurel and Oliver Hardy shot what was probably the first "talkie" in University Park. Their two-reel shot film, *Hog Wild*, features Hardy clinging to a ladder on the back of a moving truck. The last few minutes of the movie were shot almost entirely on University Boulevard (now Trousdale Parkway). The final shots, including Laurel and Hardy's car being sandwiched between two trolley cars, were shot at the intersection of University and West Thirty-fourth Street; in the background, you can see Stoops Library (now the University Club), the academic services building and the Joint Educational Project house, all of which are still standing today.

Ten years later, another legendary comedic team filmed at almost the exact same location. The Three Stooges had previously been guests at USC as part of the 1933 homecoming festivities, and in 1940 they shot their short film *No Census, No Feeling* on campus. After creating mayhem during a football game on Bovard Field, Larry, Moe and Curly flee the scene onto

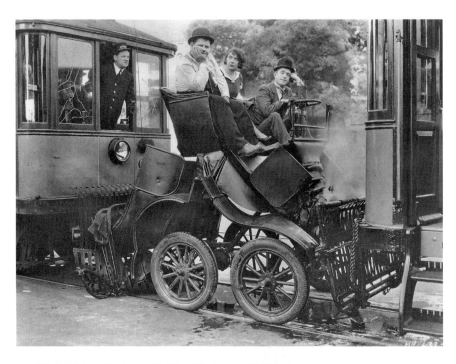

Above: A publicity still from Stan Laurel and Oliver Hardy's 1930 comedy, *Hog Wild*. The film's final scenes were shot along University Avenue, including the climactic crash depicted here, which took place at the intersection of University Avenue and Thirty-fourth Street. University Avenue's trolley cars also make appearances in Harold Lloyd and Buster Keaton films from the 1920s.

Left: The Three Stooges—Larry, Moe and Curly—pose on USC's Bovard Field during the filming of 1940's *No Census, No Feeling*. The movie's final scene features the Stooges being chased onto Thirty-fourth Street. Today, no trace of Bovard Field remains.

Thirty-fourth Street, with the United University Church visible in front of them. Followed by the entire football team, they continue to run east, toward the site where Laurel and Hardy had created their own brand of chaos a decade prior.

LATER FILMS

The first real blockbuster to be shot in the area was 1933's *King Kong*. After Kong is captured on Skull Island and transported back to New York City, he is set to be presented to the public in a Broadway theater. However, in front of a packed house, Kong breaks loose from his chains when he sees photographers' flashbulbs and wreaks havoc through the streets of Manhattan. The interiors of the theater were actually shot at the Shrine Auditorium using a split-screen technique; the audience was shot separately from a miniature model of Kong, and then the two shots were combined to make it appear like Kong was actually on stage in the theater. The stage of the Shrine would be used again in 1954's *A Star Is Born*, featuring Judy Garland. During the filming, the cast and crew took advantage of the Shrine's attached exposition hall for costuming and catering.

Few movies were shot at USC during the 1940s; notable exceptions are 1942's *The Pride of the Yankees* (starring Gary Cooper), which used USC as a stand-in for Columbia University, and 1949's *It Happens Every Spring*, featuring Ray Milland and Jean Peters. In 1954, two science fiction movies were filmed at USC's centrifuge lab, which was built for research during World War II. Both *Gog* and *Riders to the Stars* used the laboratory as it was actually intended—as a simulation for pilots and astronauts.

By the mid-1960s, larger-budget films were beginning to use USC as a backdrop. Alfred Hitchcock used Bovard Auditorium in his 1966 thriller *Torn Curtain*. Stars Paul Newman and Julie Andrews can be seen riding bicycles in front of Bovard's distinctive brick arches; they're actually supposed to be at Leipzig University in Germany. The next year, USC would act as a stand-in for the University of California, Berkeley, in *The Graduate*. In an unforgettable scene, Dustin Hoffman "travels" to northern California to follow Katharine Ross. The site where he watches her forlornly is actually Alumni Park in front of Doheny Library. Hoffman watches Ross walk down the steps of the library before turning and running toward Bovard Auditorium. Today, the park (including the fountain that Hoffman sits on) is identical to how it looked in 1967.

A promotional photo from the 1933 blockbuster *King Kong*. The shots of Kong's debut in a Broadway theater were shot inside the Shrine Auditorium; filmmakers then filmed a miniature model of the ape and spliced the two images together to make it appear as if King Kong were actually on stage.

In 1974, Mel Brooks filmed one of the scenes of his critically acclaimed comedy *Young Frankenstein* at USC. Early in the film, Dr. Frankenstein (Gene Wilder) is lecturing to a class of medical students (one of whom pesters him about his grandfather's monster); the classroom is actually one of the basement rooms in Hoffmann Hall. In 1976, nine years after *The Graduate*, Dustin Hoffmann returned to USC to film part of *Marathon Man* in Doheny Library. The 1970s and '80s also saw the filming of many television shows at USC; notable series include *Hart to Hart*, *Kojak*, *The Rockford Files*, *Simon & Simon* and *Charlie's Angels*.

Since the 1990s, the number of movies filmed at USC has increased dramatically. Dedeaux Field has been used in Tom Selleck's *Mr. Baseball*, Kevin Costner's *For the Love of the Game* and Rosie O'Donnell's *A League of Their Own*. Perhaps the most famous movie ever shot at USC, though, is 1994's *Forrest Gump* (directed by USC grad Robert Zemeckis). In the film,

USC is used multiple times as a stand-in for the University of Alabama, where Forrest Gump (Tom Hanks) attends. The shots of George Wallace's famous "Stand in the Schoolhouse Door" were filmed in front of the Allan Hancock Foundation Building; Alabama's Foster Auditorium, where the incident actually took place, was built a year prior to the Hancock Building and features remarkably similar architecture. In addition, when Gump visits his friend Jenny (Robin Wright) at her dormitory, USC's Marks Hall was used. Bovard Auditorium is also featured in the scene where Gump graduates from the University of Alabama.

More recently, USC's campus has been used for such films as *Legally Blonde* (Bovard Auditorium is used as Harvard University) and *The Social Network* (Taper Hall and Salvatori Hall are again used as Harvard University), in addition to television shows such as *Gimore Girls*, *House*, *CSI: NY*, *Felicity* and *Undeclared*.

THE FOUNDING OF USC'S FILM SCHOOL

No discussion of film in University Park would be complete without talking about the history of USC's critically acclaimed cinematic arts program. Although formally started in 1929, the program can trace its roots back to the early 1920s. The honorary "King of Hollywood," Douglas Fairbanks, began taking fencing lessons from Henry Uyttenhove at the Los Angeles Athletic Club for his 1920 role in *The Mark of Zorro*. Shortly thereafter, USC president Rufus B. von KleinSmid began taking lessons from Uyttenhove as well. The two men became close friends, and began dueling frequently at the club.

When Douglas Fairbanks was elected as the first president of the Academy of Motion Pictures Arts and Sciences in 1927, two of his first priorities were laying the groundwork for what would become the Academy Awards and establishing the College Affairs Committee. Headed by Milton Sills, the College Affairs Committee immediately began working with USC to devise a curriculum for the study of cinema. Eventually, the first course offered in the spring semester of 1929, titled "An Introduction to Photoplay," would lay the groundwork for what was to become the first film school in the nation.

The first class, held on February 6 in Bovard Auditorium, even included special appearances by Fairbanks and von KleinSmid. Although initially limited to thirty-five students, demand was so high that over seventy students

The University of Southern California

IN COOPERATION WITH

The Academy of Motion Picture
Arts and Sciences

OFFERS

INTRODUCTION
TO PHOTOPLAY

COURSE BEGINS SPRING SEMESTER

1929

Left: The curriculum for USC's first film course, "An Introduction to Photoplay." First taught in the spring of 1929, the founding faculty of USC's film school featured Douglas Fairbanks Sr., D.W. Griffith and Irving Thalberg. Today, USC's School of Cinematic Arts is one of the highest-ranked film schools in the world. *Photo courtesy of the University of Southern California archives.*

Below: Douglas Fairbanks Sr., famed silent film actor and founder of USC's film school, lectures in an early film course. To Fairbanks's right is USC's president, Rufus von KleinSmid. Fairbanks and von KleinSmid first developed the idea of a film program when they would meet to fence against each other in downtown Los Angeles. *Photo courtesy of the University of Southern California archives.*

ended up taking the course that first year (there are even reports of upward of two hundred students fighting for seats at the first lecture). For the final class, students were treated to a tour of the Paramount lot and a private screening at the Academy headquarters. In addition to Fairbanks, the founding faculty for the film program included directors D.W. Griffith, William C. deMille (older brother of Cecil B.) and Ernst Lubitsch, producer Irving Thalberg and studio executive Darryl Zanuck. Indeed, it is hard to imagine a much more impressive list of Hollywood legends from the 1920s.

This first class was such a success that within a few years, the College of Letters, Arts and Sciences was offering a wider variety of cinema classes. In these early years, guest lecturers continued to be impressive, featuring icons such as Mary Pickford, Greta Garbo and Frank Capra. In 1932, USC founded the Department of Cinematography and introduced a bachelor's degree in cinema, becoming the first school in the nation to do so. By 1933, the first student film had been produced: Richard Bare (who would go on to direct shows such as *The Twilight Zone* and *Green Acres*) adapted Edgar Allan Poe's *The Oval Portrait* at MGM Studios for a cost of only $400. Closing out an important decade for the film school, A. Arnold Gillespie became the first USC alumnus to receive an Academy Award nomination for his special effects work on 1939's *The Wizard of Oz*.

By 1940, it was determined that the film program was large enough to warrant its own location on campus. The program took over the former Architecture & Fine Arts School, a trio of buildings that sat at the corner of Hoover and Thirty-fifth Streets (near the current site of Leavy Library). The run-down wooden buildings, which film students had to share with the band, were referred to by students as the "stables" due to the fact that they had housed cavalrymen's horses during the First World War. After World War II, the film school was flooded with students due to the GI Bill, sparking a huge increase in the productivity of the program. In 1947, the Department of Cinematography first incorporated television into its curriculum, further expanding its reach in Hollywood. A master's program was added a few years later, with a PhD finally coming in 1959.

The 1950s brought the Department of Cinematography to the forefront of the movie industry in Los Angeles. Arguably the most famous class offered by the department, CTPR 480 (for which students have to direct their own short films), was introduced in 1951; it is still offered each year by the department. In 1955, the short film *The Face of Lincoln* became the first USC-produced film to win an Oscar. In the same year, a student by the name of Art Clokey released a three-minute claymation movie called

Gumbasia (a play on Disney's *Fantasia*). The film impressed producer Sam Engel so much that he provided funding to Clokey for another project—the first episode of the beloved TV show *Gumby*.

RECENT FILM SCHOOL HISTORY

The 1960s were perhaps the most infamous time for USC's cinema school. Beginning midway through the decade, USC was home to the "Dirty Dozen"—twelve film students who would change the face of Hollywood forever. Foremost amongst them was a student named George Lucas, who begun his studies at USC in the fall of 1964. As a graduate student and teaching assistant in 1967, Lucas directed a short film called *Electronic Labyrinth: THX 1138 4EB*. That year, he took first prize at the National Student Film Festival, and four years later he would expand the fifteen-minute short into his first feature film: *THX 1138*. One of the aspiring filmmakers who viewed Lucas's short at the festival was Steven Spielberg, who was ironically rejected by USC twice.

One of Lucas's roommates at USC, and another member of the Dirty Dozen, was Randal Kleiser. Kleiser, who even acted in one of Lucas's student films, would go on to direct movies such as *Grease*. Another of Lucas's close personal friends at USC was Howard Kazanjian. Lucas and Kazanjian both met their future wives at USC and would often double date together. The two men stayed very close after graduation; Kanzanjian became the vice-president of production at Lucasfilm in the 1970s and '80s, and he was both the executive producer of *Raiders of the Lost Ark* and the producer of *Star Wars Episode VI: Return of the Jedi*.

The other nine members of the Dirty Dozen also made invaluable contributions to Hollywood. Screenwriter John Milius co-wrote *Dirty Harry* and *Apocalypse Now*, while Walter Murch won an Academy Award for his sound editing on *Apocalypse Now*. Hal Barwood co-wrote *Close Encounters of the Third Kind* and went on to work as a video game designer for LucasArts. One of the most famous USC film graduates is Robert Zemeckis, who directed everything from *Who Framed Roger Rabbit* to *Forrest Gump* to the *Back to the Future* trilogy (which were co-written and produced by classmate Bob Gale). Dirty Dozen members also include Matthew Robbins (screenwriter, *Close Encounters of the Third Kind*), Caleb Dechanel (cinematographer, *The Right Stuff* and *The Passion of the Christ*), Robert Dalva (editor, *The Black Stallion* and

Jurassic Park III) and Willard Huyck (screenwriter, *American Graffiti* and *Indiana Jones and the Temple of Doom*).

In 1976, the Eileen Norris Cinema Theatre was constructed near Founders Park. The 341-seat theater, today used for film screenings and classes, is perhaps best known as the place where THX audio was first developed and installed by Lucasfilm employee Tomlinson Holman in 1983. Today, the theater is still equipped with THX, and Holman is currently a professor of film sound at USC.

Despite how prominent the Cinema Department had become at USC, it still remained nestled within the School of Dramatic Arts. In 1983, however, the film program finally split from theater and became a fully independent school within the university: the School of Cinema-Television. The year after this newly achieved autonomy saw the construction of an entirely new complex on campus to replace the "stables." With a design supposedly reminiscent of a 1930s movie studio, five buildings were constructed around a central sunken patio—the George Lucas Instructional Building, the Harold Lloyd Motion Picture Sound Stage, the Johnny Carson Television Center, the Marcia Lucas Post-Production Building and the Steven Spielberg (later John Williams) Music Scoring Stage. These buildings (with the exception of the George Lucas Building, which was demolished in 2009), are now used by the Thornton School of Music.

Now an independent school with brand-new facilities on campus, the film program continued to flourish. The 1990s saw the establishment of the Alma & Alfred Hitchcock and Ray Stark Chairs for the Study of American Film, as well as the David L. Wolper Center for the Study of the Documentary. In 2001, the Robert Zemeckis Center for Digital Arts was opened on Figueroa Boulevard, just north of campus, concurrent with the establishment of the Interactive Media Division of the cinema school. USC's videogame-design program is consistently ranked among the top in the nation.

A new era for the USC School of Cinematic Arts began on September 19, 2006, when George Lucas announced that he was donating $175 million for a new film school to be constructed. Allegedly unhappy with the architecture of the 1984 complex, he personally helped to design the new buildings. Warner Bros., 20th Century Fox and the Walt Disney Company donated an additional $50 million toward the facility. Ground was broken on October 4, with Lucas himself donning a hardhat and shoveling dirt. The first of the buildings opened in 2009, and the complex currently consists of seven buildings (including the George Lucas and Steven Spielberg Buildings, soundstages and instructional buildings). The Academy of Motion Picture

USC's new School of Cinematic Arts complex features a life-sized statue of Douglas Fairbanks, Sr., founder of USC's film program, in its central courtyard. Fairbanks was also the president of the Academy of Motion Picture Arts and Sciences when the first film class was taught at USC in 1929.

Arts and Sciences Courtyard features a life-sized statue of none other than Douglas Fairbanks, paying homage to the forces that helped to found the school back in 1929.

Chapter 9

VISITORS TO UNIVERSITY PARK

Presidents in University Park

USC was founded at a critical time in Los Angeles's history; in 1880, the city was just beginning to modernize and expand. Quickly, the university and surrounding neighborhoods became a cultural hub, attracting many special guests and events. In the 1920s, this prominence became even more pronounced with the constriction of venues such as the Shrine Auditorium and Coliseum. To this day, University Park continues to hold an extraordinary number of speeches, concerts and other events.

Amongst USC's numerous visitors have been a number of U.S. presidents. Surprisingly, the first president to visit the West Coast of the United States wasn't until 1880, when Rutherford B. Hayes took a train to California and the Pacific Northwest. Arriving in Oakland on September 9, 1880 (coincidentally the anniversary of California's entrance into the country), he spent the next few weeks visiting places such as San Francisco, Yosemite, Seattle and Portland. At even o'clock in the morning on October 23, 1880, Hayes finally made his way into Los Angeles. His trip south had been preceded a few days earlier by a visit from General William Tecumseh Sherman.

At 10:30 a.m. that day, President Hayes reached Agricultural (now Exposition) Park, where he was greeted by two hundred citizens. He was then shown the city's best livestock at the racetrack in the park. Immediately after, he was given a private tour by university president Marion Bovard of

USC's sole building, which had just been opened six weeks earlier and was still surrounded by fields of mustard. Hayes was reportedly impressed and remarked that he expected great things for the fledgling university.

The next time a president would visit USC's campus wouldn't be for another fifty-five years, when Franklin Delano Roosevelt made an appearance. On September 30, 1935, Roosevelt gave an address at the dedication of the Hoover Dam (then called the Boulder Dam) on Lake Mead. He was scheduled to spend the next day in Los Angeles before continuing south on October 2 to make an address at the California Pacific International Exposition in San Diego. While in Los Angeles, he came to the university to receive an honorary degree from President von Kleinsmid. Roosevelt, who was always cautious not to let the public know about his debilitating bout with polio, managed to walk himself up the steps of Bovard Auditorium to accept his doctorate.

A somewhat apocryphal story follows about what happened next. The next day, the *Daily Trojan* ran the headline "FDR Receives Drive-In Degree," prompting an outraged President von KleinSmid to take the matter up with Cecil Carle, the paper's editor. Apparently, a number of years later, Carle was a member of FDR's press staff and mentioned the event to the president (including von KleinSmid's outrage). Roosevelt found the story amusing and asked for a copy of the article so he could frame it on his wall.

The next time a president would make a stop in University Park came on October 20, 1958, when President Dwight D. Eisenhower gave an address for radio and television at the Shrine Auditorium. Other attendees that evening included Senator William F. Knowland and Governor Goodwin Knight.

Opposite, top: President Dwight D. Eisenhower gives an address for radio and television at the Shrine Auditorium in 1958. This was only the third time a president had visited University Park, following Rutherford B. Hayes and Franklin D. Roosevelt. Since Eisenhower, a majority of presidents have visited University Park at some point. *Photo courtesy of the University of Southern California archives.*

Opposite, bottom: A plaque in front of Doheny Library marks the site where Senator John F. Kennedy addressed students from twenty-eight colleges in 1960. Vice President Richard M. Nixon was also a speaker that day. Only a few months prior, Kennedy had accepted the Democratic nomination for president at the Los Angeles Memorial Coliseum.

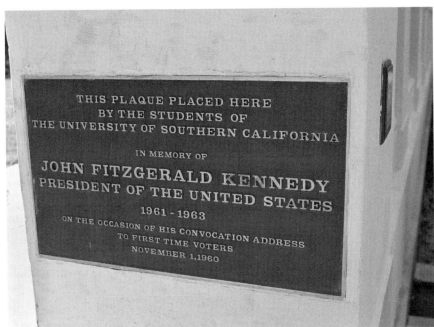

THIS PLAQUE PLACED HERE
BY THE STUDENTS OF
THE UNIVERSITY OF SOUTHERN CALIFORNIA

IN MEMORY OF

JOHN FITZGERALD KENNEDY
PRESIDENT OF THE UNITED STATES

1961 - 1963

ON THE OCCASION OF HIS CONVOCATION ADDRESS
TO FIRST TIME VOTERS
NOVEMBER 1, 1960

Another high-profile presidential event took place on November 1, 1960. A First-Time Voters Convocation was held on the front patio of Doheny Memorial Library, featuring both presidential candidates at the time—Senator John Fitzgerald Kennedy and Vice President Richard M. Nixon. An estimated fifteen thousand students turned out for the event, representing not only USC but also twenty-seven other colleges in Southern California. A plaque in front of Doheny Library still marks the site where Kennedy addressed the students.

Only a few months earlier, from July 11 to 15, the Democratic National Convention had been held across the street at the Los Angeles Memorial Sports Arena. Adlai Stevenson II, born just blocks away in North University Park, and Lyndon Johnson both announced their intentions of running, but neither could match the strength of Kennedy's campaign team. JKF accepted the nomination on July 13, and on July 15, he delivered his acceptance speech at the adjacent Los Angeles Memorial Coliseum (this speech would later become known as his "New Frontier" speech).

Although Nixon would lose the 1960 election, he again became linked to USC in 1975, when he granted the *Daily Trojan* his first interview after resigning in the wake of the Watergate Scandal. In April of that year, editor in chief Kari Granville spoke to the former president, who was at the time considering setting up his presidential library at the university. Granville later recalled that "he was sweating" during the interview.

In 1976, Gerald R. Ford ran for reelection after only a little more than two years in office. On October 7 of that year, he made a campaign stop at USC following a debate in San Francisco the previous night. Standing in front of Doheny Library (where Kennedy and Nixon had spoken sixteen years prior), Ford received a USC letterman jacket from running back Ricky Bell. There is a plaque commemorating the site of the speech opposite the Kennedy plaque.

President Ford continued to have a good rapport with USC and, in particular, the university's president, John R. Hubbard. Ford and Hubbard made a wager on the 1977 Rose Bowl game, and following USC's defeat of Michigan, Ford mailed Hubbard an autographed ten-dollar bill. Following his loss to Jimmy Carter, Ford returned to USC on two occasions in 1977 to guest lecture in numerous classes.

Perhaps no president has as close of a connection to USC as the nation's fortieth president, Ronald Reagan. In 1966, Reagan gave one of his most famous speeches, "The Creative Society"; it was this speech that he used to formulate his campaign for governor that same year. Following his ascension to

Gerald R. Ford made a stop at USC during his 1976 reelection campaign. He was presented a letterman jacket from running back Ricky Bell. Later in life, Ford maintained a friendship with USC president John R. Hubbard. Today, a plaque marks the site where Ford spoke. *Photo courtesy of the Los Angeles Times archive.*

the presidency, Reagan stayed a "frequent visitor" to USC, stopping by campus before officially opening the 1984 Olympic Games and giving his first post-presidential speech at USC. The former president also celebrated his seventy-eighth birthday in Bovard Auditorium in 1989, featuring a performance by the Trojan Marching Band and a student-led rendition of "Happy Birthday."

What is even more interesting is the relationship Ronald Reagan had with USC's leaders. Deemed his "kitchen cabinet" (in reference to Andrew Jackson's unofficial advisors in the 1830s), Reagan had a group of friends and businessmen in California who advised him on many decisions. Amongst these men were USC board officers and donors Walter Annenberg, Robert Fluor and Henry Ford Salvatori (names that will be familiar to any USC student), in addition to USC president Norman Topping.

More recently, President Barack H. Obama spoke to a crowd of thousands in Alumni Park on October 20, 2010, remarking, "This is a Trojan kind of welcome. Fight on!"

Other Notable Events

Many other notable individuals have spoken at USC. In 1956, architect Frank Lloyd Wright (who had previously spoken at USC's Harris Hall in 1940) spoke regarding his exhibition titled "Sixty Years of Living Architecture."

Undoubtedly one of USC's most famous alums was Neil Armstrong, best known for being the first man to walk on the moon on July 21, 1969. The very next year, after his retirement from space travel, Armstrong attended USC to finish his master's degree in Aerospace Engineering. On May 13, 2005, almost thirty-six years after his famous moonwalk, he returned to USC to deliver the commencement speech to the graduating class in Alumni Park.

Since University Park has multiple large venues, many musicians and bands have played concerts in University Park. One of the most legendary, and earliest, came on June 8, 1956, when Elvis Presley took the stage for his first Los Angeles concert. Having played California for the first time only two months earlier, the Shrine Auditorium show failed to even warrant a review in any of Los Angeles's newspapers. Today, however, it is one of the venue's most fondly remembered events.

Many more concerts soon followed: the Velvet Underground played two shows in 1968, and the Grateful Dead played shows in 1967, 1968 (one of which was released as a live album, *Two From the Vault*), 1976 and 1978. Pink Floyd played two nights of its "Saucerful of Secrets" tour in July 1968 at the Shrine, and a Jimi Hendrix concert in February 1968 infamously got the promoter banned from the venue after an image of a naked woman was shown on a screen behind the band.

Other notable performances have included Ray Charles in 1964, Buffalo Springfield in 1967, Frank Zappa in 1968 and 1974, Fleetwood Mac in 1969 and 1974, King Crimson in 1974, Rush in 1974 and 1975, ELO in 1974, Genesis in 1975, Blue Öyster Cult in 1975 and KISS in 1975. One of the more infamous events at the Shrine Auditorium occurred on January 27, 1984. Michael Jackson, at the peak of his fame, was filming a Pepsi commercial on stage when pyrotechnics malfunctioned and set his hair on fire, giving him second-degree burns on his scalp.

The Shrine Auditorium has always been a popular venue for awards shows, particularly the Academy Awards. The first time the Academy Awards was held there was on March 13, 1947. The host that year was Jack Benny; presenters included Ronald Reagan, Shirley Temple and Billy Wilder; and *The Best Years of Our Lives* won seven awards, including best picture, director and actor. The following year, on March 20, *Gentleman's Agreement* would take home the award for best picture.

Left: Arguably the most famous architect of all time, Frank Lloyd Wright made two visits to USC's campus, in 1940 and 1956. Here he is seen with USC president Rufus von KleinSmid in Bovard Auditorium at his traveling exhibition titled "Sixty Years of Living Architecture." *Photo courtesy of the Los Angeles Public Library.*

Below: The famed Elvis Presley meets with adoring fans backstage before his 1956 concert at the Shrine Auditorium. This was the first time Elvis would play in Los Angeles, and the city's newspapers didn't even cover the event. Since the 1950s, the Shrine Auditorium has been the site of hundreds of concerts by artists like KISS and Pink Floyd.

The Academy Awards was held at the Shrine Auditorium ten times between 1947 and 2001, bringing many of Hollywood's elites to University Park. The Shrine Auditorium has also been the host of sixteen Grammy Awards. In recent years, the Shrine's usage has dropped off significantly; however, there has been recent talk about bringing the Oscars back to the venue. *Photo courtesy of the Los Angeles Public Library.*

The Academy Awards wouldn't be held at the Shrine again until April 11, 1988, when the Sixtieth Academy Awards took place there. That year, *The Last Emperor* would win nine awards; a highlight of the night was Audrey Hepburn and Gregory Peck's reunion onstage thirty-five years after the release of *Roman Holiday*. For the following decade or so, the location of the awards alternated between the Shrine Auditorium and the Dorothy Chandler Pavilion downtown. The Sixty-first Academy Awards, held on March 29, 1989, is notable for being the last public appearance of Lucille Ball, who would pass away less than a month later.

Other Academy Awards that were held at the Shrine were the Sixty-third Academy Awards (March 25, 1991; best picture went to *Dances with Wolves*), the Sixty-seventh Academy Awards (March 27, 1995; best picture went to *Forrest Gump*), the Sixty-ninth Academy Awards (March 24, 1997; best picture went to *The English Patient*), the Seventieth Academy Awards (March 23, 1998; best picture went to *Titanic*), the Seventy-second Academy Awards (March 26, 2000; best picture went to *American Beauty*) and the Seventy-third Academy Awards (March 25, 2001; best picture went to *Gladiator*).

The Grammy Awards was held at the Shrine Auditorium sixteen times between 1978 and 1999, which is more than any other venue. Other award shows that have used the Shrine Auditorium include the Primetime Emmy Awards, the American Music Awards, the People's Choice Awards and the Screen Actors Guild Awards. However, the Staples Center nearby, which opened in 1999, has become a more popular venue for both concerts and awards shows in recent years.

The Los Angeles Memorial Coliseum has also seen its fair share of big-name performers. Among the more notable are the Bee Gees in 1973; Pink Floyd in 1975 and 1988; Jethro Tull in 1976; Journey in 1979 and 1980; Van Halen in 1979 and 1988; Aerosmith and Rick James in 1979; Black Sabbath and Yes in 1980; the Rolling Stones (with Prince opening) in 1981; the Clash in 1982; The Who in 1982 and 1989; Bruce Springsteen in 1985 and 1988; U2 in 1987 and 1997; Metallica in 1988, 1992, 2000 and 2003; and the Rolling Stones again in 1989 (this time with Guns 'n' Roses as an opening act).

The third major concert venue in the neighborhood, located right next to the Coliseum, is the Los Angeles Memorial Sports Arena. Although not as new and state-of-the-art as some of Los Angeles's venues, it has always been a personal favorite of Bruce Springsteen, who played there thirty-two times between 1980 and 2012. Another memorable string of shows took place between February 7 and 13, 1980, when Pink Floyd played on its "The Wall" tour. Los Angeles was one of only two cities the band would play in the United States, the other being New York a week later. Roger Waters re-created the performance in 2012 at the Coliseum, playing to a sold-out crowd.

Other notable performances at the Sports Arena have come from the Beach Boys in 1963 and 1973; the Rolling Stones in 1965; The Who, Van Halen and Yes in 1980; Ozzy Osbourne in 1981; AC/DC in 1982; U2 in 1982, 1985, 1987, 1992 and 2005; Aerosmith in 1986; David Bowie in 1987 and 1990; Def Leppard in 1987; Michael Jackson in 1989; the Red Hot Chili Peppers in 1989; Madonna and Billy Joel in 1990; and Nirvana and Pearl Jam in 1991.

It is impossible to list all of the other significant events that have been held at the Shrine Auditorium and Los Angeles Memorial Coliseum, and only a brief number can be covered here. In 1964, a "Project Prayer" rally (supporting prayer in schools) featured an impassioned speech from film legend Gloria Swanson. On the night of July 3, 1970, jazz legend Louis Armstrong threw a birthday party at the Shrine, which continued until the following morning.

On January 20, 1938, American author Sinclair Lewis spoke at the Shrine Auditorium. Lewis, best known for his books such as *Main Street*, *Babbitt* and *Arrowsmith*, was the first American to be awarded the Nobel Prize for Literature in 1930. His speech at the Shrine was titled "Propaganda and Poppycock"; when asked what the American people could do to fight propaganda, he replied, "Let every individual kick like hell."

At the Coliseum, significant events include speeches by Charles Lindbergh, General George S. Patton and Nelson Mandela; the first-ever papal Mass by Pope John Paul II; and a 1963 Billy Graham Crusade that drew 134,254 people.

Perhaps the most famous non-human visitor to USC's campus was a stray mutt by the name of George Tirebiter. One day, in 1941, a group of students noticed a black and tan dog, perhaps part Airedale, lingering near Currie's Ice Cream Parlor, which was located at Hoover and Jefferson Boulevards, behind the United University Church. The students noticed he was scrounging for food and chasing cars. Someone noted an apparent similarity in appearance to a fellow student, hence the given name "George." It was his habit of chasing cars along University Avenue that gave him his surname. George quickly became a member of the Trojan family, beloved by the thousands of fans who came to know him.

A series of events led to further infamy for Tirebiter. At a home football game versus UCLA, USC's mutt bit the nose of rival mascot Joe Bruin. Soon after, at another game, he chased after Berkeley's Golden Bear mascot.

USC's original George Tirebiter, a stray mutt that was embraced by the student body and inducted as the school's mascot. Tirebiter was a staple at USC home football games from 1941 to 1950 and was even the victim of multiple "dognappings" by rival UCLA students. Today, a statue on Trousdale Parkway commemorates the beloved dog. *Photo courtesy of the University of Southern California archives.*

Perhaps as revenge, George was kidnapped in October 1947 by UCLA students. On November 1, 1947, the *Los Angeles Times* released a photo of George with the letters "UCLA" shaved in his fur. The following year, Tirebiter was held captive by UCLA students for eleven days. After the "dognapping," he was immortalized by having his pawprint dipped in wet cement at the north end of campus, alongside USC football stars. Tirebirter's pawprints are still on display in USC's Tutor Campus Center.

By 1950, time had taken its toll on George, and he retired to a farm in El Centro, California. Unfortunately, he continued his old habits, and within a year he was tragically run over by a car while chasing it. A funeral procession was arranged down University Avenue (now Trousdale Parkway) in honor of the fallen mascot. In 2006, a statue of Tirebiter was unveiled at the southern end of Trousdale, to commemorate the mutt's former stomping grounds.

Shortly after the passing of George Tirebiter, student government replaced him with a local puppy that bore a striking resemblance to his predecessor (leading some students to dubiously speculate that it was Tirebiter's son). George Tirebiter II, as he came to be known, was the subject of at least two "dognappings" before his retirement. Tirebiters III and IV came in 1953 and 1957, with neither lasting more than a year as mascot.

Following Tirebiter IV, USC students decided that dogs were no longer working out as mascots. The current Trojan mascot, a white horse named Traveler, was introduced at USC's home opening football game in 1961. During this first season, the costume worn by the horse's rider was the same costume that Charlton Heston wore in 1959's *Ben Hur*. For twenty-eight years, the horse's rider was Richard Saukko, who owned the original Traveler (named after Robert E. Lee's horse during the Civil War). At the time of this writing, Traveler VII, a purebred Andalusian, is the current mascot.

SELECTED BIBLIOGRAPHY

Daily Trojan, various issues.

El Rodeo Yearbook, various issues.

Epting, Chris. *Los Angeles Memorial Coliseum*. Chicago, IL: Arcadia, 2002.

Henley, W. Ballentine, and Arthur E. Neelley. *Cardinal and Gold*. Los Angeles: General Alumni Association, University of Southern California, 1939.

Los Angeles Times, various issues.

Reynolds, John H. *The Trojan Gallery: A Pictorial History of the University of Southern California*. Los Angeles: University of Southern California, 1980.

Roseman, Curtis C., Ruth Wallach, Dace Taube, Linda McCann, Geoffrey DeVerteuil and Claude Zachary. *A University and a Neighborhood: University of Southern California in Los Angeles, 1880–1984*. Los Angeles: Figueroa, 2006.

Sloper, Don. *Los Angeles's Chester Place*. Charleston, SC: Arcadia, 2006.

ABOUT THE AUTHOR

B orn in Santa Monica and raised in Huntington Beach, California, Charles Epting is currently an undergraduate student at the University of Southern California. He is studying history, geology and environmental studies and for several years has been a volunteer at the Los Angeles County Museum of Natural History, studying paleontology.

Visit us at
www.historypress.net
· ·
This title is also available as an e-book